The New Sermon Slot (Year A)

Sharon Swain is a former teacher, Diocesan Adviser on religious education, and Diocesan Evangelism Adviser to the Diocese of Worcester. She now has two rural churches, and is a Rural Dean in the Diocese of St Edmundsbury and Ipswich. She is the author of several highly successful SPCK books, including *Conversations with God*, the two *Christian Assemblies for Primary Schools*, and *Reach Out*.
The New Sermon Slot volumes for years B and C are also available.

D1427714

THE NEW SERMON SLOT

All-Age Ideas
for the Common Worship Lectionary
(Year A)

SHARON SWAIN

Published in Great Britain in 2001 by
Society for Promoting Christian Knowledge
Holy Trinity Church
Marylebone Road
London NW1 4DU

British Library Cataloguing-in-Publication Data

A catalogue record for this book is available from the British Library

ISBN 0–281–05192–5

Typeset by Wilmaset Ltd, Birkenhead, Wirral
Printed in Great Britain by
The Cromwell Press, Trowbridge, Wiltshire

Contents

INTRODUCTION

The New Sermon Slot (Year A), like *The New Sermon Slot (Years B and C)*, is based on the Common Worship Lectionary three-year cycle of readings used by many churches. It aims to give those who are responsible for organizing all-age worship some suggestions for incorporation into the normal framework of their service, as part of the Service of the Word within the Communion Service, or the 'sermon slot' in the Family Service.

The book allows for a wide variety of situations, and encourages leaders to tailor the suggestions to suit their own individual needs. The ideas are based on the readings in Year A of the Common Worship Lectionary, allowing leaders to adapt them to suit their circumstances in a practical way, whether that is for adults and children, or adults alone. *The New Sermon Slot* is primarily a book of practical suggestions that allows worship leaders to expound more fully the word of God. Some notes are included for leaders to enable them to add a comment, and these can be expanded to suit local circumstances.

☐ *The Family Service*

The 'family' or 'all-age' service reminds us that we are all on a journey of pilgrimage together. Children and adults need each other to progress along the path, and to learn and worship apart can hinder their progress.

The traditional family service must no longer be a children's service, or indeed a time when the church pays lip service to its children. The family service, whether it is eucharistic or not, must take account of all ages in the church.

The organizers of the family service face a challenge to occupy the adults' minds (and often, though not always, their maturer understanding of the faith), as well as the children's desire to worship with their whole body.

The New Sermon Slot gives ideas for those faced with the challenges of conducting all-age services. It uses the traditional teaching point of the service to allow congregations to stop and look at the message of Jesus Christ and at their response.

☐ *The All-Age Service*

For those who wish to get the most out of this book the following suggestions might be helpful:

- All-age services need a *team* of people to organize them. Do not expect one person to do it all.
- All-age services need *advance planning* and *prayers*. Think and plan at least four or five weeks ahead to get the best out of the service.

- All-age services must be *flexible*. Anything can – and often does – happen when those who take the service are using modern methods of education. You may also need to tailor the instructions to suit your circumstances, and double the number of groups or dispense with some. But with the Holy Spirit's help, and good planning, even difficulties can be turned to your benefit.

- All-age services are for *everyone*. You cannot always keep the two-year-old occupied and neither should you expect to all the time, but there should be something for every age in the service.

- All-age services are for *equals*. Never talk down to children or new adults in church. They may know more than you, or be spiritual giants. Equally, don't expect those who have been worshipping for 50 years to know all the answers, for they won't.

- The reason for learning in such a practical and experiential way is not about 'getting back to childhood'. It is important that everyone has the opportunity to learn more about their faith, and we learn best by what we see, hear *and* do!

- All-age services need the *goodwill* of some people. If flak occurs don't give in, but do question whether you went too fast at first. Don't threaten anyone by asking them direct questions, or by making them take part. Take things slowly and don't try to change everything overnight.

- All-age services are *fun*. Learning about God can be fun as well as instructive. So enjoy yourself.

Note: The text of the New RSV (Anglicized) version has been used throughout the book.

THE FIRST SUNDAY OF ADVENT

Jesus reminds us that the Son of Man will return, unexpectedly, to gather God's chosen people. On that day one person will be taken and another left. Are we ready for this to happen today?

Isaiah 2.1–5
Romans 13.11–14
Matthew 24.36–44

- Large number of soft objects to pass around the group (e.g. a beanbag, small teddy, or small ball of wool).
- An instrument to make a very loud sound (e.g. cymbals, an organ, or a keyboard).
- Paper or craft-foil.
- Scissors.
- Star pattern.
- Pencils.
- Large board or wall, and a dark-blue sheet on which to hang the stars.
- Glue or pins to hang stars.
- *Optional:* One very large star.

☐ *Starter*

Create small groups of mixed-aged people. If possible the groups should find some space to stand or to sit in a circle, though this is not essential, as pews can be used. Invite the groups to create relationships within the groups. Perhaps they are a family, or just friends, or members of a football team. It is important that a real situation is imagined.

Now give each group three or four soft objects to pass around, e.g. beanbags, small teddies, or balls of wool. Many different objects can be used as long as they are easy to hold in one hand.

Finally invite everyone to think of some *action* that implies work, e.g. hammering, sewing, cleaning, painting, etc. and then to perform the action. The actions might be appropriate to the whole family or team (e.g. putting up the tent for camping, or playing a game of football), and people may speak to one another. At the same time, however, the beanbags (or whatever have been used) are to be passed around the group.

Inform everyone that they should stop when they hear a loud

noise. Allow the action to occur for some time so that people really get into their role play, and then create the loudest noise possible, e.g. crash some cymbals, or play the organ *fortissimo*. At this point everyone stops their work action, and those holding the beanbag are asked to leave their group and move away to one side.

Inform everyone that those who have left the group are those who have been 'taken' (as in the Gospel reading), and ask them the following questions:

- How do members of the group feel about losing members of their family or team?
- How do those who have been taken away from their family and friends feel?
- How do people feel about the unexpectedness of what happened?
- How do people feel about the lack of warning that they were to be separated from one another?
- Invite them to discuss this with each other for a few moments, and listen to any feedback from the groups.

Invite everyone to go back to their seats.

☐ *Comment*

The Gospel reading for today, as well as the passages either side of this section of St Matthew's Gospel, appear to speak of the Second Coming of Jesus (though there is some debate as to whether they refer to the forthcoming destruction of Jerusalem which was to happen in AD 70), though Jesus never actually uses the phrase, 'Second Coming', himself.

To the Jews the notion of a time when God would intervene in history to restore his kingdom was a common one. The phrase 'the Day of the Lord' was often used for this idea. The Christian writers saw this as the time when Jesus would intervene to rescue God's people. We are not told where they are to go, or what is to happen to those who are left. We can presume that this group will be with God, and the other group will remain outside his presence. Surely this latter must be a notion of hell.

But the purpose of this parable is to remind us that we must be ready for when God intervenes. We must never be so involved with the material things of this world that we forget the spiritual things. We must never be so preoccupied with this world that we forget to watch for the coming of God. In Noah's time the people ate and drank, and did not see what was on the horizon. Only Noah prepared for the flood that was to come.

We are called to a state of wakefulness this Advent, and reminded that when the Lord comes, he comes with a shattering speed to judge all peoples. The question is how shall we change our lives this Advent to make ourselves ready for God's coming?

☐ *Conclusion*

Give everyone a large star, at least 15–20 cm in diameter (a large version of the star is in the Appendix). If possible these should be cut from white paper or silver craft-foil (not domestic foil which is thinner). Before the service prepare a large sheet of dark blue paper to cover a wall in the church or a large board. The paper is to hold *all* the stars. To save time in preparation these could be cut out before the service.

Invite everyone to write one thing they intend to change in their life this Advent. Make sure that the intentions are small enough to be possible. (For example: Each week I will visit my next-door-neighbour who is unwell.) Over the next few weeks the congregation will be adding to this, so space needs to be left to write three more intentions. Encourage everyone to write their first name or something that will identify their star next week. The following Sunday invite people to find their star before the beginning of the service, to save time.

The stars can be placed on the wall with the promises showing or hidden. If craft-foil is used the promises should be placed on the back. Above the stars place a large title: OUR ADVENT PROMISES.

☐ *Optional*

Place a very large star on the board or wall to represent the star that led the Wise Men to Bethlehem, and as a reminder to the congregation to look forward at this time of the year.

THE SECOND SUNDAY OF ADVENT

God's kingdom of love and peace has been initiated by Jesus, but we are responsible in the way we live our lives, for helping to bring the kingdom to fruition.

Isaiah 11.1–10
Romans 15.4–13
Matthew 3.1–12

> - Copies of the Old Testament reading for the congregation.
> - OHP or flip chart and fat pen.
> - *Optional:* newspapers.
> - 1 or 2 old bed sheets.
> - Whistle.
> - *Optional:* Pencils and some spare stars, as well as glue or pins.

☐ *Starter*
Remind the congregation of the description of God's peaceful kingdom and of its King, as described in the Old Testament reading. If possible make copies of the reading for everyone to see. Explore what is different about this description when compared to our world today.

Then make two lists (one after the other) on an OHP or flip chart, to show what is good and bad about our world. Head one 'Good in our world' and the other 'Evil in our world'. There may well be duplicate words or phrases on the two lists, as some things can be both good and bad depending upon their use.

☐ *Optional*
Use newspapers to identify good and bad in our world.

☐ *Comment*
Isaiah prophesies the destruction of God's people, the Jews, because of their disobedience. But just when all seems lost he makes a new prophecy. Imagine the royal line of King David as a tree, he says. From that stump a new shoot will grow. All is not lost. The line of corrupt kings has ceased, but now a new king will arise who will follow in the tradition of Jesse, the father of David.

Another prophet offering the Jews some hope at this time is Micah. He refers to someone who will come to be a ruler over all

Israel, and who will be a special ruler. He is to be wise and understanding, full of power and strength, and more importantly he is to 'fear the Lord'. He is to be a man of God, whose task is to protect the poor and the downtrodden. Isaiah also picks up this theme, describing the kind of reign that this king will introduce. It is to be one of peace and prosperity, where both people and animals live together in harmony.

If all this sounds a little far-fetched (with animals becoming vegetarians!) we need not become too concerned with the minute details. But Christians have taken this passage to refer to the kingdom of God initiated through the birth, death and resurrection of Jesus. God's kingdom has started but it is not completed. It is up to us as Christians to forward the work of God's kingdom. We can do that by living our lives in the way that God wants us to live, so that God's kingdom of love and peace will gradually be brought into our world.

□ *Conclusion*

Lay a large sheet on the floor and invite eight people to come and give a practical demonstration of how we should live in this world. Instruct the group that they are to stand somewhere on the sheet, and they are to stay there until you blow a whistle. Should anyone step or fall off the sheet, then the game is over and all must leave. The aim is to keep everyone on the sheet for as long as possible.

At first there will be plenty of room for all, but the situation will soon change. Now ask the eight to step off the sheet ('It's OK, there's no trick, I just want to make the sheet smaller!'), and fold the sheet in two. Everyone steps back onto the sheet and this time there is less room. After a moment blow the whistle, congratulate them all, and fold the sheet in half again. Continue folding the sheet and inviting them to stand on it, until someone falls off and the game is over.

You might want to hold a trial run until people get the idea that as it gets smaller they have to help one another stay on the sheet. Alternatively you could use two different sheets and two groups, and challenge them to see who can keep going the longest. Discuss what happened with the congregation.

- How did the group survive?
- Who helped the most?
- What happened to small children/elderly people?
- Did the group work together?
- What was the most difficult thing?

Remind the congregation that if God's peaceful kingdom is ever to occur fully (as shown in the picture that Isaiah gives us), then we must begin by working together, and by thinking about each other, in the way we have just seen. Comment that each one's good affects the good of the whole.

□ *Optional*

Continue to make a second Advent promise by writing an 'intention' on the stars (see last week).

THE THIRD SUNDAY OF ADVENT

The apostle James advocates that the new Christian community should wait in patience for the coming of Jesus. This message is as strong today as it was in the first century AD.

Isaiah 35.1–10
James 5.7–10
Matthew 11.2–11

- OHP or flip chart.
- Paper and fat pens.
- Two large notices: 'No patience' and 'Lots of patience'.
- *Optional:* A list of the stories on a flip chart or OHP.

☐ *Starter*

Place two very large notices up at either end of the church (e.g. at the east and west end of the main aisle, or on the east or west wall). One notice should say 'No patience' and the other 'Lots of patience'.

First talk with the congregation about the meaning of patience. Make sure that all the children understand the meaning of the word. Ask questions like:

- What makes you cross?
- How do you feel when a smaller child/brother/sister upsets your jigsaw or interrupts a game?

Acknowledge that some people have more patience than others, and that everyone's patience is tested by different things. What upsets one person may not upset another.

Now invite everyone to stand in the aisle(s) along the length of the church. Call out different situations and ask people to stand somewhere along the line between 'No patience' and 'Lots of patience' according to how they feel tested by the situation. (You might need to carry out a practice run.)

- (for adults and teenagers) Someone pushes into the queue for the bus ahead of you.
- (for adults) No other car will let you out of the cul-de-sac onto the main road.
- (for children) Your brother or sister ruins your game with your friends.

7

- (for adults) On ringing a large company you keep getting an automatic voice that says, 'If you want . . . press 2, if you want . . . press 3, etc.'
- (for adults) The washing line breaks and someone offers to mend it. The first time you put out the washing, it breaks again and all the clothes get muddy.
- (for children) Your brother or sister (or friend) borrows something of yours and when it is returned you find it is broken.
- You make a special point of going to the library as your books are overdue by a few days. You discover the library is closed.
- You miss the last bus by two seconds and see it disappearing into the distance.
- (for children) You spend a long time painting a picture, but someone else in the family throws it out, thinking it is rubbish.

□ *Comment*

Patience is an underrated virtue. We are more accustomed to venting our anger if something upsets us, rather than counting to ten. The example of 'road rage' is all too normal now. Indeed some people seem to believe they have the right to shout and be rude to others if they are upset.

St Paul says that patience is one of the fruits of the Spirit (see Galatians 5.22). In other words it is one of the outcomes that we can expect to see in a person's life when they are living a life in tune with God. It is also one of the signs of true love. Paul reminds us that 'Love is patient' (see 1 Corinthians 13.4). When we truly love another person we do not lose our patience with them.

In today's epistle reading, James is speaking to the new Christian community about another kind of patience. He says that they need to wait patiently for the coming of the Lord. This is a community activity. The people are to be like a farmer who after his seed is planted waits patiently for the growth of his precious crop. The people of God are to show the same kind of patience in the way they live their lives together. They must treat one another with gentleness, and not grumble about each other.

For us, some 2,000 years after the death of Christ, this message is still important. As Christians we need to be strong and patient, believing that Jesus will return to judge the world, and that this Second Coming may occur at any time. The question is, when Jesus returns, what kind of community will he find waiting for him?

□ *Conclusion*

Working in twos, or in small groups, look at some of the situations used in the Activity. These could be put up on a flip chart or OHP, to remind the congregation of them.

Ask each group to come up with some suggestions as to how people might keep their patience in these situations. Allow the groups a few moments for discussion and then hear back from as many of the groups as required. The suggestions could be listed on an OHP or flip chart if desired.

Lastly ask the same groups how, as a congregation, they might 'wait patiently for the Lord'. What activities or actions might help make the worshipping community grow in strength, so that if Jesus appears in their lifetime they will be ready for him?

☐ *Optional*
Put the suggestions up onto a flip chart or OHP, and make a 'fair copy' for display in the church.

☐ *Optional*
Continue to make a third Advent promise by writing an 'intention' on the stars (see Advent 1).

THE FOURTH SUNDAY OF ADVENT

A study of the prophecies about the Messiah helps to teach us something about Jesus, the Messiah.

Isaiah 7.10–16
Romans 1.1–7
Matthew 1.18–25

- Bible texts and Bibles.
- Small squares of card.
- Pens.
- Large crib with straw, or large amounts of straw and a sheet of plastic.

☐ *Starter*
Divide the congregation into small groups of mixed ages. Give each group as many Bibles as possible (any edition), and one of the following lists of verses to look up. Invite them to read these traditional prophecies that look towards the coming of Jesus as the

Messiah. Invite them to write down all they can find out about the Messiah. What kind of person do the prophets imagine him to be? How will he appear? What will he do?

Prophecies 1	*Prophecies 2*
Isaiah 11.10	Isaiah 40.11
Malachi 3.2–3	Isaiah 11.1
Isaiah 7.14	Isaiah 9.6
Micah 5.2	Micah 5.4
Isaiah 42.1	Isaiah 42.2–3
Isaiah 53.4	Isaiah 53.5

Prophecies 3	*Prophecies 4*
Isaiah 11.2	Isaiah 11.2b–4
Isaiah 42.4	Isaiah 53.3
Isaiah 53.7	Isaiah 53.9
Isaiah 61.1	Zechariah 9.9
Isaiah 53.11b	Isaiah 53.12
Zechariah 9.10	Isaiah 40.5

☐ *Conclusion*

Place a large crib filled with straw where it can be seen. Alternatively make a large bed out of straw placed on plastic or a cloth for easy removal. Ask the congregation to tell you what they have discovered about the Messiah. Write up all the conclusions in note form onto small cards, and place around, or in, the crib. Use a number of scribes to help speed up the process.

Below the crib place a large notice saying, 'The Messiah'. If possible place this somewhere as a focal point for Christmas worship. You might want to leave the crib empty until Christmas Day and then put a swaddled figure in the crib.

☐ *Comment*

As we near Christmas we have a tendency to forget that we are celebrating the birth of the Messiah. We can get carried away with thinking about the baby born in a stable. The Jews had been looking forward to the birth of the Messiah for hundreds of years. Prophet after prophet had spoken of the time when the Messiah would appear. It would be a time of great change, when God would make his mark on the world.

There was real longing for this time, but although they kept a watch to see if the signs were right, few expected the Messiah to appear as a homeless child in a stable. Most thought he would be another David – a king, and a warrior. Many of the prophecies describe him as someone who comes in power to overturn the existing order. In the Old Testament reading from today from Isaiah, although the Messiah is to be born as a child, he is to bring in a reign of terror. While in a prophecy from Malachi he is described as a 'refiner's fire'. Surely, the Jews thought, this Messiah would be born in a palace?

Another group of prophecies, however, describe the Messiah as someone who will suffer for the sins of others. These 'suffering servant' prophecies in Isaiah give a completely different picture. This is no warrior king. This king will be meek and he will achieve God's promises to the world through suffering. It is this picture that emerges with the ministry of Jesus.

☐ *Optional*
Hold a discussion on how much Jesus fulfilled all these prophecies. Are we still waiting for some of the prophecies to be fulfilled?

☐ *Optional*
Continue to make a fourth Advent promise by writing an 'intention' on the stars (see Advent 1).

CHRISTMAS DAY

The story of the nativity as it appears in the Gospels is looked at again in detail, to give a fresh perspective.

Isaiah 52.7–10
Hebrews 1.1–4
John 1.1–14

- Scripts for the choral speaking.
- A conductor.
- Bibles or New Testaments.
- Paper and pencils.
- *Optional:* Card, template, and scissors to make Chrismons.

☐ *Starter*
Produce some choral speaking using all the congregation. Divide them into three groups, and give everyone a copy of the text. It will probably help if someone conducts the whole piece.

Group 1	[*quietly*] Listen!
Group 2	[*quietly*] Can you hear?
Group 3	Listen now!
Group 1	They approach!
Group 2	Their feet can be heard!
Groups 2 & 3	Listen!
	[*pause*]
Group 1	[*quietly*] Listen!
Group 2	Can you hear?
Group 3	The messengers come!
Group 1	Their feet approach!
Group 2	The messengers come!
Group 3	They come to announce!
	[*pause*]
Group 1	[*quietly*] Listen!
Group 2	Can you hear?
Group 3	They announce good news!
Group 1	[*positively*] Our God reigns!
Group 2	He reigns for ever!
Group 3	[*quietly*] Who speaks?
Group 1	How beautiful
Group 2	How beautiful are the feet
Group 3	How beautiful are the feet of them
Groups 1 & 2	Who bring good news!
	[*pause*]
Group 3	What news?
Group 1	What news do they bring?
Group 2	What news do the messengers bring?
Group 3	[*louder*] Break forth into singing!
Groups 1 & 2	What news do they bring?
Group 3	[*louder*] Sing for joy, O Jerusalem!
Groups 1 & 2	Tell us the news!
Group 3	Sing aloud!
Groups 1 & 2	[*crossly*] What news is there?
Group 3	The Lord is here!
Group 1	Where is the Lord?
Group 2	Tell us, where is the Lord?
Group 3	The Lord has saved his people! [*slower*] The Lord IS HERE!!
	[*pause*]
Groups 1, 2 & 3	The Word is made flesh, and come among us!
	[*pause*]
Group 1	We have seen him!
Group 2	His light shines!

Group 3	We have seen his glory!
Groups 1 & 2	The Word is made flesh, and come among us!
Group 3	But his own did not receive him!
Group 1	His own did not recognize him!
Group 2	His own rejected him!
Group 3	The Word is made flesh, and come among us!
Group 1	His own did not accept him! [*pause*]
Group 2	He was in the world.
Group 3	The world came into being through him.
Group 1	Yet the world knew him not. [*pause*]
Groups 2 & 3	But to all who receive him . . .
Groups 1	Who believe in his name . . .
Groups 2 & 3	He gives the power . . .
Groups 1, 2 & 3	[*slower*] To become the children of God.

☐ *Comment*

The Christmas story is one that we all know perfectly well, or do we? Where does the story of the birth of Jesus appear in the Bible? Does it appear more than once, and if so, are they the same stories?

For many of us these are difficult questions, and if we can answer them, we cannot be sure if our answers are correct. But what if we add to this a question about the different people and the different objects that appear in the story? Unfortunately the most well-known of stories has become somewhat jumbled in our minds.

So today we are going to explore the whole story of the nativity afresh, to see what we can learn again about the birth of God's Son, Jesus Christ.

☐ *Conclusion*

Divide the congregation into small groups and give each group a piece of paper and a pencil. Make sure no group has a Bible. Ask the following questions:

- How many books in the Bible contain the story of the birth of Jesus?
- Which book(s) are these?
- Between you tell the story of the birth of Jesus to each other in the group, putting it in the correct order.
- Which parts of the story come in which book(s)?
- Identify as many people and objects (e.g. manger, gifts, etc.) associated with the Christmas story. When people look as though

they have finished, or become stuck, give each group as many
Bibles or New Testaments as possible. Ask them to look up the
story, and help any groups that look lost. If necessary direct them
to Matthew 2.1–15 and Luke 2.1–20. The following are some of
the people and artefacts they should find. There may be more:

Angel	Wise Man	Gifts
Mary	Joseph	Baby Jesus
Sheep	Star	Shepherd
Manger	Throne	Herod
Innkeeper		

☐ *Optional*

The people and artefacts could be drawn onto card, cut out, and
hung on the Christmas tree, rather along the lines of Chrismon
symbols (i.e. Christian symbols to hang on the Christmas tree).

THE FIRST SUNDAY OF CHRISTMAS

Through the theme of journeys we remind ourselves of the journey
of faith upon which we all travel.

Isaiah 63.7–9
Hebrews 2.10–18
Matthew 2.13–23

- List of journeys and Bible references.
- A map of Palestine for each group.
- Paper and pencils.
- Bibles.
- A place to display the work, and pins or Sellotape.

☐ *Starter*

Look at famous journeys in the New Testament, and at the
emotions of the people who journey.

Form groups of six to eight people in mixed-aged groups.
Allocate each group a journey, a number of Bibles, a map of
Palestine, paper and pencils. Different groups may look at the same
journey.

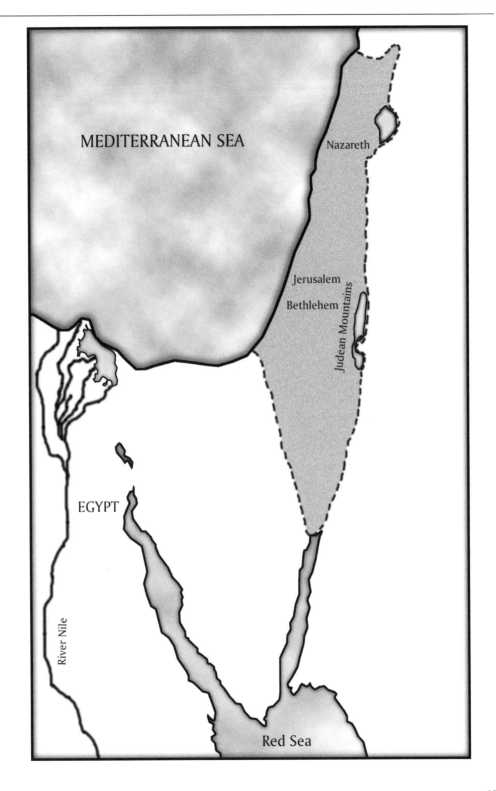

- Journey of the Wise Men: Matthew 2.1–2 and 2.12
- Journey to Egypt: Matthew 2.13–15 and 2.19–23
- Journey to Elizabeth's house: Luke 1.26–40
- Journey to Jerusalem: Luke 2.1–5 and 2.39
- Journey to Jerusalem: Luke 2.41–47

Extra journeys, if required:

- Jerusalem to Jericho: Luke 10.30–37
- Journey through Samaria: John 4.1–4, 43–46; 5.1 and 6.1

The task of each group is to draw on their map the journey taken and the likely towns that they might have passed through or stayed in. Don't forget mountains and lakes may have to be 'negotiated'. In the case of the Wise Men each group can decide a rough area of the world they might have come from and possible routes to Palestine. Lastly the group should look at who is travelling, and at the circumstances of their journey. What emotions might these people have experienced? List these emotions on a sheet of paper.

☐ *Conclusion*

Put up all the maps somewhere visible. Make sure that each has a heading and a Bible reference explaining the journey. Alongside the map put the list of characters journeying and their possible emotions.

Allow everyone sufficient time to look at the different offerings.

☐ *Comment*

Two thousand years ago travelling was difficult. The easiest travel was accomplished by boat, but this could be dangerous because of high seas and piracy. Travelling overland was slow and equally dangerous. Even within the Roman empire bandits existed, as we can see from the story of the Good Samaritan. Added to this, it was difficult to travel in the winter when the roads became impassable.

Yet despite this many people did travel, sometimes very long journeys that took weeks or even months. From our study of the Gospels today, we have looked at a few of these journeys. We have tried to imagine how the people concerned might have felt. Were they tired, excited, worried? Where might they have stayed the night, and how long would it have taken them to get to their journey's end?

At the beginning of the new year it does us good to remember that we too are journeying. We are not walking the dusty highroads of Palestine, but we are journeying in our faith. This new year will hopefully see us take steps *forward*, and not *back*. But we need to remember that each step is carried out *with* God who walks alongside us. So we need to walk in faith.

☐ *Optional*
Encourage the congregation to think about the milestones that
might be reached in this coming year in their lives (e.g. a birthday,
a child to be born, perhaps a likely death, a new job, a marriage or
relationship to be repaired, a new school). Write these down
anonymously on slips of paper, collect them, and use in the
intercessions.

THE SECOND SUNDAY OF CHRISTMAS

Our traditional notions of 'rich' and 'poor' are explored and
overturned when we think of Jesus.

Jeremiah 31.7–14
Ephesians 1.3–14
John 1.(1–9) 10–18

- Leaders who know the area or will do some work the week
  before.
- List of the areas of the world.
- OHP or flip chart and suitable pens.
- *Optional:* Picture symbols, e.g. a stable scene from a card, a
  spider, money, a crown, glass of dirty water, an empty dinner
  plate, or a beautiful item of clothing or material.

☐ *Starter*
Carry out this 'Prince and Pauper' activity. Divide the congregation
into small groups of four to six people. Double-up on activities as
desired, and offer younger children a separate activity. Allocate to
each group a leader who has done some work on one area of the
world – as a minimum they have found out some information in the
week before, but preferably someone who has visited the country
concerned. Give each group one of the following geographic areas:

- Africa
- Central America
- India
- Afghanistan
- China

- Korea
- Europe
- Australia
- Russia

If the congregation is quite small, then ask each group to look at both those who are wealthy and those who are poor in each country. Where a large number of groups are required, allocate the country and either the word 'Poor' or 'Rich'.

The task for each group is to imagine the lifestyle of someone living in their country, either as a rich person, or someone who is very poor. List as many comments as possible onto a large sheet of paper, e.g.

Central America

- Poor
- No transport
- No school
- Rains cause mudslides which kill people

When each group has finished, hang up the sheets of paper, making sure each is headed with the name of the country and whether they are looking at Poor or Rich.

Finally using an OHP or flip chart create two more lists, this time for Israel. Deliberately look at the differences that might have existed between Jesus as the son of Mary and Joseph (fairly poor) and between Herod as king (rich). Head one 'Poor' and the other 'Rich'. Take suggestions from the congregation and list them.

☐ *Optional*

Hide symbols (in picture form if this is easier) to show examples of 'Rich and Poor' around the church, and allow younger children to search for them. Examples might be:

- A stable (from a Christmas card)
- A spider
- Money
- A crown
- Glass of dirty water
- An empty dinner plate
- A beautiful item of clothing or material, etc.

☐ *Comment*

The truth about Christianity is not always apparent to those who do not wish to see it. It is about God who sends his son to earth, a son who is not born in pomp and circumstance with all the trappings of this world; a son whose existence is not trumpeted to the world; a son who will not ride on a white charger and lead his people into traditional battle. This was what the Jewish world expected.

Instead, Jesus is born into humble circumstances, to a carpenter and his wife on a night when they have had to travel far to register with their enemies the Romans. So instead of a comfortable, warm home, he is born in a stable with the animals, still no doubt warm, but not so comfortable.

Yet despite everything seeming to be wrong, for Christians it is not so. For if we look again at the story we shall see who is rich and who is poor.

 □ *Conclusion*

Refer back to the two lists made for Jesus and for Herod (the 'Rich' and 'Poor' lists). Now begin to overturn the original conclusions. First, change the headings over, so that Poor now sits over the description of Herod in his palace, and Rich now sits over Jesus born in a stable.

Explain that all is not what it seems. Look at the categories written and show that what seems like poverty is in fact richness. Jesus might have been born into physical poverty, but what he offered was pure gold. Jesus was in fact the king, though he lived in poverty. Herod living in great splendour was in fact living in great spiritual poverty and was doomed.

Refer to the lists you have hung up. Comment that many of the people living in such poverty in our world are rich in the spiritual blessings. For example, the church in Africa is growing faster than anywhere else in the world. Whereas in the West, society is all too often spiritually dead. It may be rich in material terms, but it is very poor in spiritual terms.

EPIPHANY

God's word spreads throughout his world to all peoples, and its manifestation shows itself slightly differently in each century and in each country.

Isaiah 60.1–6
Ephesians 3.1–12
Matthew 2.1–12

- Large star.
- Large blue sheet or blue frieze paper.
- Crib.
- Scissors.
- Pencils or pens.
- Smaller pre-cut stars, or white or silver paper and star templates, or use those made before Christmas.

□ *Starter*

Use the church's crib scene as the focal point for this activity. Before the service create a very large star and hang it high above the crib scene. If there is already a star hanging over the crib, of a sufficient size, this can be used as the focus material.

Behind the crib scene hang a large blue sheet or piece of blue frieze paper. Give out star templates (or create the stars beforehand) and silver or white paper. The stars should be at least 10 cm across (see Appendix A). Also give out pens or pencils.

In the week before the service appoint group co-ordinators and give them the task of finding some information about people who have heard about Jesus in the last 2,000 years, and/or the different ways this has expressed itself. Use local libraries, or search the Internet for information. Any of the following areas would be suitable:

- Look at saints (e.g. New Testament saints or others through the ages) and how their faith changed their lives.
- Look at the different Christian traditions (e.g. Greek Orthodox, Church of England, Roman Catholic, Russian Orthodox, Coptic, etc.).
- Look at the different reformed traditions (Lutheran, United Reformed, Baptist, Pentecostal, etc.).

The group co-ordinators might like to introduce the subject by sharing what they have discovered themselves, and then broaden the discussion by asking questions such as:

- How did these people hear about Jesus?/Who took Christianity there?
- What kind of Christianity is worshipped in this/these countries?
- What are the strengths of this denomination or church?
- Are there differences between our worship and theirs?

Keep the discussion positive. The aim is to thank God for the way that he spread the message of Jesus throughout the world, not for concluding that one denomination or way of worshipping is better than another.

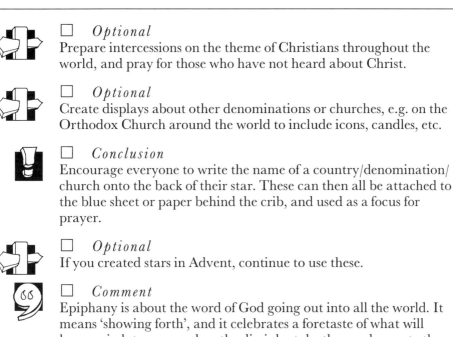

☐ *Optional*

Prepare intercessions on the theme of Christians throughout the world, and pray for those who have not heard about Christ.

☐ *Optional*

Create displays about other denominations or churches, e.g. on the Orthodox Church around the world to include icons, candles, etc.

☐ *Conclusion*

Encourage everyone to write the name of a country/denomination/church onto the back of their star. These can then all be attached to the blue sheet or paper behind the crib, and used as a focus for prayer.

☐ *Optional*

If you created stars in Advent, continue to use these.

☐ *Comment*

Epiphany is about the word of God going out into all the world. It means 'showing forth', and it celebrates a foretaste of what will happen in later years when the disciples take the good news to the world. The Wise Men are not from Israel, they come from much further away, and they in their turn will take the good news back to their countries. For Christianity is not to be just for the house of Israel as we know. God was sending his message to the gentiles as well as to the Jews.

As such we should not be surprised at the way the good news has been taken and explored in different ways across the globe over two millennia. It is surely a strength and not a weakness that men and women can worship their Creator in different ways. Instead of seeing the different denominations as a weakness we should begin to regard them as a strength. For we can learn so much from each other, and without these differences our faith is diminished. In the same way we have so much to learn from the saints who went before us. Their faith, their ordinariness, and their experiences all teach us how to live the Christian life.

THE FIRST SUNDAY OF EPIPHANY

God's plan involves the whole world. Whether or not they accept his servant, God's hand of love is never withdrawn.

Isaiah 42.1–9
Acts 10.34–43
Matthew 3.13–17

- Two teams of people to carry out the role play.
- Two places to use (e.g. chancel and the back of the church, or two rooms).
- 3 or 4 copies of the Two Towns: Task Sheet.

☐ *Starter*

Create two fairly large teams of people to carry out some role play, and then send them to separate parts of the building (e.g. the chancel and the back of the church, or opposite corners of the room), or to other rooms if there are some available.

Give the following instructions to the two groups.

THE TWO TOWNS: TASK SHEET

You are all people living in a beautiful town situated in the mountainous region of the Tyrol.

- First, decide what name to give your lovely town, and appoint a mayor [*maximum 1–2 minutes*]. Now send the name of your town and its mayor to the worship leader.

Unfortunately, your town is being oppressed by another town on the other side of the mountain.

- Create a list of all the dreadful things that the other town has done to you (e.g. attacked visitors to the town, stopped the water supply to the town, etc.) [*maximum 1–2 minutes*].
- Now decide what you are going to do about the other town to ensure that you are safe from oppression in future. [*You should be as ruthless as you like – the role play needs some imagination here!*] [*Maximum 2 minutes*]

While the two groups are working through the Task Sheet continue with the remainder of the congregation. This group is to play the part of the judge (i.e. God). Inform them that they have to solve a terrible situation that has arisen in the area. Two towns in the Tyrol are locked into conflict. Things have been bad for many years, and it looks as though outright war is about to break out. How can they stop this happening?

Finally impose some restrictions on the judge:

- He has to work through human beings.
- He cannot impose all-out war, because these two towns are sovereign territories.

Inform the congregation that it is unlikely that the towns will listen to the judge (after all, people don't listen to God).

Now come up with a strategy to deal with the two towns. This might include sending them messages, or even sending someone to them as a mediator.

When the towns send their names and the names of their mayors to the worship leader, make sure that the other town is given the same information.

When the time is up, hear back from the two towns, keeping them in opposite corners (since they will obviously want to harangue each other!). Ask each mayor what their complaint is and what they intend to do about it. Keep an eye on the time!

□ *Conclusion*

Now place the whole problem before the congregation who are acting as judge. What are they going to do? Encourage them to carry out their plan of action (e.g. sending someone to the two towns) and see what happens. Keep the role play going. Is there a possible satisfactory end, or will the towns destroy one another?

□ *Comment*

[Adapt the following according to what happened in the role play.] God out of his love seeks to bring us back to himself for we are separated and estranged from God. So he sends his beloved Son to carry out the rescue package. Isaiah says:

> Here is my servant . . . my chosen, in whom my soul delights;
> I have put my spirit upon him;
> he will bring forth justice to the nations. (Isaiah 42.1–2)

Christians believe that this servant was none other than Jesus himself, who was sent as a mediator to a wicked and wayward world to bring it back to God.

But we know what happened. Although some people listened and were changed, too many ignored his words. They refused to listen, and they preferred to go their own way. Finally nothing but his death would satisfy them.

We have seen how easy it is to refuse mediation and to go our own way, and then there is no way back. For we have dug a hole of our own making. The only difference with God is that the one who mediated, Jesus, never stops offering us an opportunity to change.

THE SECOND SUNDAY OF EPIPHANY

An exploration of the word 'Mission' leads to some practical work.

Isaiah 49.1–7
1 Corinthians 1.1–9
John 1.29–42

> - OHP or flip chart and pen.
> - Group leaders.
> - Bibles.
> - A good dictionary.
> - Mission work sheets for all the congregation.
> - Pencils.

 □   *Starter*

Brainstorm the word 'mission' onto an OHP or flip chart. What does this word mean to the congregation?

If desired, invite someone to come and talk about mission and what it means to them or to their church. Explore who carries out mission, and how.

Then divide into small mixed-aged groups of, say, eight to ten people. Allocate a question to each group. You may need to appoint group leaders beforehand, and some groups may require Bibles. The leaders should have some skills in helping people contribute to the discussion.

- What do you think your mission is in the church? (The group may come up with a number of ideas.) What one thing can you do this month that would help you to achieve this goal?

- What was the mission of the new church in the Acts of the Apostles (see Acts 2). How did they achieve it? Can you apply some of their techniques today? What one thing can you do this month that would help to achieve this goal?
- What do you think is the mission of your church? Can you come up with 15 words that describe it? Is this mission being achieved at present? What one thing can you do this month that would help to further this?
- What do you think mission work is all about? Make a list of six essentials for mission work to happen. What one thing can you do this month to help further this?
- What do you think is the difference between evangelism and mission? Is your church carrying out mission work and evangelism? You might need a good dictionary! List what work it does and think about its effectiveness. What one thing can you do this month to help this work?

☐ *Optional*

Look with children at practical examples of mission work, e.g. how do we tell others about God, how do we invite people to come to church, and how do we care for others in our world? Examples could be found from newspapers and magazines and a collage created.

☐ *Conclusion*

Provide each person with a pencil and a sheet headed 'Mission work'. The sheet should have space for writing and at the bottom of the page words from Matthew 28.19–20.

Give everyone time to write down the one thing that they can do to help mission work in the church this month. Encourage adults to work with children. The sheets should then be collected and offered to God at an appropriate moment in the service. They could be left on the altar for the following month as a reminder of what has been promised.

☐ *Comment*

John the Baptist was the greatest of evangelists. His task was to bring the people back to God; and to warn them of the coming of the Messiah. His whole life was dedicated to carrying out God's task and bringing the people to repentance.

We are all called to evangelize, that is to tell people about God. We don't find it easy, but God calls us to spread his word. We are his hands, his feet, and his mouth. We are the means that God chooses to spread his gospel. This is a task given to each one of us.

If 'evangelism' is the spreading of the word of God, then 'mission' is the wider work of God. We are involved with mission when we help our neighbours, when we raise money for a Christian charity, when we teach in Junior Church, or when we help raise the profile of Christian work across the world. We are all called to spread the word and to mission in God's world.

THE THIRD SUNDAY OF EPIPHANY

True commitment only comes when someone is willing to give up all that they have for God; true unity only comes when a group is willing to give up everything for the sake of peace.

Isaiah 9.1–4
1 Corinthians 1.10–18
Matthew 4.12–23

- OHP or flip chart, paper and pen.
- Copy of the story.
- 23 people (old man and donkey, woman and 3 daughters, and 17 donkeys).
- Paper and pens for groups.

☐ *Starter*

Using an OHP or flip chart put up a piece of long division, e.g. 120 divided by 20. Using simple language (so that young children might at least understand the concept) work out the sum. This could also be followed by doing a piece of long division using people as the numbers in the sum, e.g. divide six people by two people, or by including a piece of long division that doesn't completely work out evenly.

Emphasize that all that is happening in division is that a large number of numbers/people are being divided into 2, or 20, etc. parts.

Now tell the following story.

THE OLD MAN AND HIS DONKEY

Once upon a time there was an old man who owned a donkey. He loved this donkey more than anything in the world. He talked to it; he curled up beside it on cold nights; and it carried him and his belongings when he was tired.

One day the old man met a woman who had three daughters. Now the woman had 17 donkeys. She was very rich! The woman wanted to divide her donkeys between her three daughters so that they had a fair share. She wanted her oldest daughter who did most of the work to have a half share of her donkeys. She wanted her second oldest daughter, who didn't do quite as much work to have a one-third share of her donkeys. And she wanted her youngest daughter, who did little work, to have a one-ninth share of her donkeys. The problem was it just wouldn't work out.

[Now physically show everyone how it doesn't work, by using people (23) as the old man and his donkey, the woman and her 3 daughters, and the 17 donkeys. If you don't have enough people, one person could carry a card saying '17 donkeys'.]

Seventeen donkeys just cannot be divided in half, at least not without killing one of the donkeys, and this wouldn't do.

[Encourage everyone to think of a solution.]

Suddenly the woman sees the old man and his donkey, and she has an idea. Would the old man let her have his donkey? She asks him if she can have his donkey. The poor old man is very upset to lose his beloved donkey, but he sees that the woman has a problem, and finally he decides to help her out by giving up the only thing he possesses – his donkey.

Now the division will work!

[Divide the 'donkey' people into three groups: one half (9 people); one third (6 people); and one ninth (2 people).]

But amazingly there is still one donkey left. The old man who gave his donkey away can have his donkey back!

[Leave the brilliant mathematicians to try and work out why this is – it will keep them occupied for the rest of the day!]

☐ *Comment*

Jesus called the disciples to follow him. This was no part-time appointment which they could leave when things got difficult. They had to commit themselves for life. They gave up everything, wives, families, and jobs to follow him into an unknown future.

We may not be called to make this kind of commitment in our lives. We may be called to live a faithful life and carry out the life of a Christian in the place where we live and work. But the church does need those who will give up everything if it is to be faithful to its charge. It needs priests and bishops, it needs evangelists and missioners, and we should continue to pray that men and women will feel called to give this kind of commitment to God.

Then there is another kind of giving. There are still many divisions between the different Christian traditions. If these are ever to be resolved it will be because one group feels able to give up everything that it holds dear in order to achieve unity. After all God gave up his Son to the cross in order to rescue us.

☐ *Conclusion*
Take an issue that is prevalent in the church or society and explore the different positions. Divide into small groups and give each group an issue for discussion, for example:

- Evangelicals/Catholics are the only Christians on the right path.
- Homosexuality.
- Children should be seen but not heard in church.
- The priority for all Christians is to give away their money/ concentrate on God.
- It is better to start with charities at home than to give to overseas charities.

The more 'hot' the topic, the better. Ask each group to look at *both* sides of the issue and come up with the main arguments for each viewpoint. Write these onto a large sheet of paper.

Now ask the groups to consider the questions again, this time to try and come up with solutions that might be acceptable to both sides of the argument.

Finally, comment that if this was impossible, remember that the division of the donkeys only worked because the old man gave up everything.

THE FOURTH SUNDAY OF EPIPHANY

Jesus works with the things of this world to teach people about the way that God works.

1 Kings 17.8–16
1 Corinthians 1.18–31
John 2.1–11

> - Bibles or copies of the story of the wedding at Cana.

□ *Starter*

Divide the congregation into mixed-age groups. You might want to appoint co-ordinators to help the groups. Give each person a copy of the story of the wedding at Cana from a modern Bible. Their task is to:

- Read the story through again, carefully taking note of all that happened.
- Decide how many characters there might have been in the story (e.g. Jesus, the couple getting married, Jesus' mother, disciples, the steward of the feast, etc.).

At this point give each group the name of one person or group of people who were at the wedding. Now ask them to look again at the story, but this time from the perspective of that person or group.

- What two questions would they like to ask of another person or group, or what two things would they like to say to another person or group?

It would be helpful if not every group wanted to ask a question of Jesus. Encourage groups to ask questions of the bridegroom and the steward of the feast, as well as Jesus. An example of the kind of questions that might occur, are:

- (to the disciples) Why aren't you out teaching the people about God, instead of attending a feast?
- (to Mary) Why don't you leave your son alone, he's only enjoying himself?
- (to Jesus) Why are you wasting your gifts by turning water into wine?

□ *Comment*

To many outside the church, Christians seem to be 'po-faced' and 'holier-than-thou'. One of their main complaints is that we are no better than anyone else, so why should we go to church, and we are such kill-joys, always saying 'Don't do that!' To some extent they are right. We don't appear very cheerful sometimes, though they miss the point that we go to church exactly because we are no better than anyone else, and there are things happening in our world we would prefer to change.

But if we look at Jesus we see a man who was involved in the ordinary things of life. He had meals with his friends, he went sailing, he walked miles, and in today's story he is at a family or friend's wedding. He liked good friends, wine and laughter. It wasn't all doom and gloom. Neither should it be for us. Jesus brought us a message of great hope that should leave us feeling carefree and joyful.

The other thing to notice from this incident is that Jesus used the ordinary things of life to teach people about the way that God works. He used stories about wheat and tares (weeds), or shepherds and their sheep, to talk about the things of God. The miracle of the wedding at Cana is another such example. It is the first major sign of his power. The writer of St John's Gospel says it is 'the first of his signs . . . and revealed his glory'.

□ *Conclusion*

Brainstorm thoughts on what this exercise has taught you about Jesus, about this story, and about miracles in general, write ideas onto an OHP or flip chart.

Alternatively send two people from each group to another group, e.g. two from the 'Jesus' group should go to the 'Mary' group, etc. Now ask some questions of those who have just joined the group. Keep it positive, and do not make the 'newcomers' feel under attack.

PROPER 1

Jesus said Christians are the salt of the earth. How should this affect the way we live our lives?

Isaiah 58.1–9a (9b–12)
1 Corinthians 2.1–12 (13–16)
Matthew 5.13–20

- Grapefruits.
- Sugar.
- Spoons.
- Plates.
- Memos.
- Pencils.
- *Optional:* Coffee with no sugar; homemade lemon drink with no sugar; porridge with no sugar.

□ *Starter*

Produce a grapefruit cut up to eat, but with no sugar on it. Make sure the grapefruit is as sour as possible. Now invite a number of people to try the grapefruit. Mention how delicious it is.

After the tasting, enquire what is wrong with it. All will probably mention the sourness of the grapefruit. Ask them how it can be improved, and then add some sugar to the grapefruit. Get the volunteers to taste another mouthful, and ask if it has improved.

If desired, offer a number of items that need something to improve their quality, e.g.

- a cup of coffee with no sugar to someone whom you know prefers it with a lot of sugar.
- a cup of instant porridge (using some warm milk or water from a thermos), with no sugar or syrup on it, to someone with a sweet tooth.
- a drink made from fresh lemons and water, but with no sugar in it.

Choose your volunteers carefully, to ensure that all find the food or drink distasteful. In each case add sugar and invite the volunteer to try the food or drink again.

 □ *Comment*

We have seen something of what it is like to taste something that is sour or bitter without sugar. Sugar (and for that matter salt) are essential ingredients of our diet, although many of us try to cut

*How can we act
as salt in the world?*

Jesus said:
'YOU ARE SALT TO THE WORLD'

down on them for various health reasons. But the thought of food without any sweetener like sugar (or honey, or syrup), or meals without salt ('Imagine chips with no salt!') doesn't appeal. Our meals would seem so bland.

Jesus says that Christians are the salt of the earth, and if the salt is ruined then it needs to be disposed of and thrown away. This is a really strong criticism of many Christians. We are to be like salt (or sugar). We are to add flavour to the community. Where there are active Christians, the community will be affected. That doesn't mean that the community will be all sweetness and light, for where there is good there is often evil. But active Christians make a difference to a community, by keeping their vision wide and broad; by reminding others of the things of the kingdom; and by working always to achieve the goals set forth by Christ.

If this feels like a tall order, it is! But we were not put here to live a life of idle luxury, concerned only for ourselves. We are there to further the kingdom of God in this place.

 ☐ *Conclusion*

Before the service create some small 'memos' and give one to each member of the congregation, along with a pen or pencil.

Invite everyone to work together in twos or in small groups and produce some practical suggestions as to how as Christians they can have an effect upon the world.

Write the suggestions down onto their memo. These should be taken home and displayed somewhere they will be seen, or perhaps used as a bookmark, to be reflected, and acted, upon in the coming weeks.

PROPER 2

Jesus teaches that to think a sin is the same as actually carrying out the sin. We should ask forgiveness of each other and of God.

Deuteronomy 30.15–20
1 Corinthians 3.1–9
Matthew 5.21–37

- Large sheets of paper and fat pens.
- Drawing pins or Pritt-Tak to hang the sheets of paper.
- *Optional:* Words of the Peace.

☐ *Starter*

Try to ensure that the confessional element of the service is held after the sermon slot this week.

Create small groups of mixed ages, and give each group a large sheet of paper and a fat pen. Their task is to think of as many sins as possible, and write them up on the large sheets of paper. The sins should be those that all of us commit from time to time, e.g. pride, laziness, gluttony, etc., and things such as murder and adultery.

When the groups have finished writing up all the sins, place the sheets of paper all around the church. If there is no wall space, hang them from seats or pew ends, or anywhere else within reach of everyone.

☐ *Comment*

Jesus teaches the people with authority, in a way that the scribes and Pharisees have never been able to do. The law of Moses is so revered that all they can do is to repeat what it teaches, but Jesus interprets the law afresh. The people are astonished at what he says, and the Pharisees and scribes are angered at his words.

To the astonishment of the disciples and those listening, Jesus teaches that it is as wrong to think about committing a sin, as it is to actually carry it out. Indeed we shall be judged if we are angry with our brother or sister, or if we have insulted them. It is important that we ask for forgiveness of the person that we have sinned against, and that we confess our sin, before we come to God's altar. Jesus says:

> 'So when you are offering your gift at the altar, if you remember that your brother or sister has something against you, leave your gift there before the altar and go; first be reconciled to your brother or sister, and then come and offer your gift.' (Matthew 5.23–24)

It is important to note that we must be reconciled *first* to the person we have sinned against, and only *then* to God. We cannot avoid asking forgiveness from our friend or brother/sister, by simply asking forgiveness of God. We must carry out both actions.

□ *Conclusion*

Now give everyone a pen or pencil and ask them to walk round the lists and tick every sin that they themselves have committed over their lifetime. If people do not want some sins to become public, you could always have an 'Unknown Sin' box to be ticked.

Finally, ask the congregation to go and tick again, any sin that they have committed this last week, that is, as yet, unconfessed.

□ *Optional*

Now say the words of the Peace:

Leader   The peace of the Lord be always with you.
All   And also with you.

All now offer a handshake or a kiss and say the words of the Peace. Follow this by saying the words of the general confession and asking God's forgiveness.

PROPER 3

For a house to be stable it needs firm foundations. Christians need Jesus to be in their lives, as a firm foundation.

Leviticus 19.1–2, 9–18
1 Corinthians 3.10–11, 16–23
Matthew 5.38–48

- Lego.
- Table.
- Bible or copies of 1 Corinthians 3.10–11, 16–23.

□ *Starter*

Using as much lego as possible create a building. This could be partially built beforehand, though it should not be fixed to a Lego base. Ensure there are windows and doors to the house. The house should be fairly unstable.

Place the house onto a table or flat surface, and invite people to help with the building, making it into a substantial 'villa', with as many eccentricities as the builders like.

□ *Comment*

While the builders continue with their task (preferably without talking to each other) continue talking.

St Paul teaches us in 1 Corinthians about faith. Our faith is built on a foundation, he says, and that foundation is Jesus Christ himself. He thinks of Christians as houses. If the house has no foundation, if it is not deeply rooted in the ground, then eventually at the first problem it falls down. It doesn't matter what wonderful materials we use to build our house, if that first foundation is not properly in place, the house will never last.

Our faith is rooted and built on Jesus Christ. Others, teachers and leaders, help us to build on that initial faith as we continue through our lives. If we remain true to our initial faith things will be well, but if at some time we stray from our footings, we cannot expect our house to stand. As we mature we need to make sure that we are still building on the foundations laid many years ago.

[Now look at the house that the builders have been building. How stable does it appear to be? Can it survive long without a base (its foundation)?]

□ *Conclusion*

Set up a number of different groups, doubling up topics as needed. You might wish to appoint group leaders before the service, to do some thinking, and to bring the appropriate materials. There might also be multiple groups, as needed. All groups will need to study the Corinthians reading first.

□ Group 1

Look at the Corinthians reading, then create some art work that shows how strong your church can be when it bases all its work on Jesus. This might be a mural or a diagram drawn onto a flip chart. Take some of the work carried out by the church and show how it might be improved. Perhaps new work would be initiated if the church were to get back to basics and follow the commands of Jesus. Keep the tone of the discussion positive, rather than negative.

□ Group 2

This group might be composed of children with one or two adults. As a group build a new house out of Lego, this time fixed to a base for stability. The group should also look at the Corinthians reading.

☐ **Group 3**

Working as a group, initially, explore the Corinthians reading. Then break into two's or work as individuals, and explore how life would change if Jesus was put first in every part of life. Write down some of the changes that would be experienced, and from the list resolve to make at least one change from now on.

☐ **Group 4**

Look at the Corinthians reading then explore the instabilities of life. On a large sheet of paper make a list of some of the things that are wrong with society, and then with your part of society. This might mean looking at your town or village, or your church or school. Can this group make one single change to their society or environment? Or, alternatively, can they make a list of prayer subjects from their discussions?

Hold a brief plenary session to hear back from each group. What has been discovered or learnt about the foundations of our faith?

THE SECOND SUNDAY BEFORE LENT

Jesus teaches of the pointlessness of worrying, and of the need to trust in God for all our needs.

Genesis 1.1—2.3
Romans 8.18–25
Matthew 6.25–34

- A pair of scales.
- OHP or flip chart.
- Small pieces of paper for the congregation.

☐ *Starter*

Before the service find a large pair of old-fashioned scales, where the weights are placed on one side to balance the item being weighed. Put them where they are visible to everyone.

Give everyone in the congregation a small piece of paper headed 'Things I worry about' and a pencil. Encourage small children to work with adults. Allow two or three minutes for everyone to write down the things that worry them. People might wish to talk together about their worries, or prefer to keep them to themselves. Either is acceptable.

When the lists are completed, ask everyone to come forward and place their sheets on *one side only* of the scales. There should be no weights on the scales at this time so that the scales will sink with the weight of the paper.

Now discuss with the congregation the kind of things (in general) that worry them. Using an OHP or flip chart make a list of the most worrying. You could make a Top Ten list, if desired. Many of the following may well come up:

- Money
- Children
- Death
- School
- Dentist
- Elderly relatives
- Having a baby
- Work, etc.

☐ *Comment*

Worry is a natural part of life, it seems. We worry over many things from going to the dentist to our own death; we get in a stew if we are likely to be late for a meeting or if we don't achieve what we expect to achieve. In some ways worry is acceptable. If we didn't worry at all, we would never avoid danger. It is a part of our safety mechanism to be concerned about danger, for instance, and it can help keep us safe.

However, worry has become the curse of our age. It has got out of hand. It is at the root of all stress, which causes high blood pressure and heart attacks. It also hinders healing in those with major illnesses like cancer. For Christians it is also a sign of lack of faith.

Jesus reminds us in St Matthew's Gospel that worry is pointless. We cannot live one day longer by worrying. It achieves nothing positive. He reminds us that the birds of the air do not grow crops and store grain in barns, yet God cares for them. Neither do flowers in the field, which may only flower for one day, and then are gone.

Jesus says that God cares for us and he will give us what we need for the work he has given us to do. It is more important that we concentrate on God's kingdom and on bringing justice to our world. In essence, worry is after all a kind of selfishness!

☐ *Conclusion*

Give everyone another slip of paper, the same size as that which they have previously used. Encourage them to turn from thinking about their worries to thinking about their blessings. What is it that they have to be thankful for? What is good in their life? Some of the following may come up:

- My family
- My health
- The beauty of nature
- That I have food
- My friends, etc.

Now ask everyone to come forward and put their pieces of paper onto the scales. The two sides should balance if the paper was of the same size and there was the same number. [*Have two extra sheets ready in case!*] Point out that we may have worries but that these are balanced by the joys in our life, for which we thank God.

☐ *Prayer*

Give thanks for all the good things in our lives.

THE SUNDAY NEXT BEFORE LENT

We can live by going from fortune-teller to fortune-teller to decide what we shall do with our lives, but we would do better to consult God.

Exodus 24.12–18
2 Peter 1.16–21
Matthew 17.1–9

- 1 large Oracle.
- 1 square of paper for each group.
- Pens.

□ *Starter*

Before the service make your own large-scale 'Oracle' card.

Take a large square of plain white or coloured paper (at least 50 cm). Fold the paper in half, and then into quarters. Open out the sheet. Now fold each corner to the centre, before turning the square over to the flat side. Fold this last square in half twice, vertically and horizontally. Now open the Oracle and write on different segments, as shown in the example.

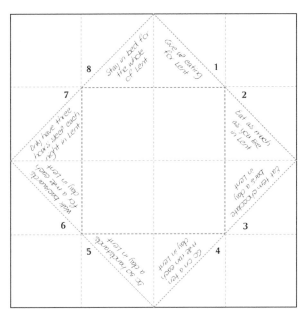

Write these numbers on the outer segments: 1, 2, 3, 4, 5, 6, 7, 8
Write the following on the centre segments:

Give up eating for Lent.
Eat as much as you like in Lent.
Eat ten chocolate bars a day in Lent.
Go on a ten-mile run each day in Lent.
Do 30 handstands a day in Lent.
Walk backwards for a mile each day in Lent.
Only have three hours sleep each night in Lent.
Stay in bed for the whole of Lent.

Work the oracle by putting thumbs and forefingers in the flaps and pushing them together, first one way and then the other.

□ *Comment (1)*

Remind the congregation that Lent starts next week. Lent is the time when many people decide to give up things. Ask whether people have thought about what they might do this Lent. Listen to some of the suggestions.

Comment that in Old Testament times people could go to an Oracle and ask for guidance. Sometimes this was a special holy man or woman, as with Apollo's shrine in Greece. Even the Hebrew nation could communicate with God in this way. The high priest held the Urim and Thummin. We are not entirely sure what they were, perhaps they were some kind of stones. What we do know is that they were worn by the high priest and were used by the king to communicate with God, although they gradually went out of use after the destruction of the second temple.

Suggest that you might be able to help people with the decision they must make about how they will observe Lent. Now invite seven or eight people (adults and children) to try out your Oracle. Ask them first to choose a number, and then open up the inner triangle to read what they must do this Lent.

The congregation will obviously find some of the oracles amusing, but point out that no one should follow these instructions as some of them (e.g. 'Give up eating', or 'Eat ten chocolate bars a day') could be very dangerous.

□   *Conclusion*

Invite the congregation to break into groups of about six to eight people. These can be mixed-age groups, or alternatively children might like to work together with the help of an adult.

Give each group a square of paper and ask them to create their own Oracle. The difference will be that their Oracle will have sensible suggestions for Lent inside. Groups should endeavour to come up with their own suggestions, but in case there is a problem keep a list of suggestions to hand.

□   *Suggestions:*

- Join a Lent group.
- Read a passage from the Bible each day.
- Attend a midweek service.
- Attend church every Sunday.
- Visit someone who is unwell or lonely.
- Say my prayers morning and evening each day.
- Give some (more) money to charity.
- Offer help to a friend or family member.
- Read a book about God or about the Bible.

Encourage each member of the group to have a go and see what their Oracle suggests they should do in Lent. You might wish to hear back from the groups as to the suggestions that they thought up, and whether members might want to take up the suggestions in Lent.

☐ *Comment (2)*

Next week sees the start of Lent. Many of us make Lenten promises, to give something up, or to take on something. However, before we do so this year we need to use today's Gospel reading to help us reflect on what we are intending to do and why. Jesus has come to a turning point in his ministry. From the passage before today's reading in St Matthew's Gospel, we can see that he knew he was treading a road that would lead to his death. He says to his disciples, 'If any want to become my followers, let them deny themselves and take up their cross and follow me.' There is no doubt what lies ahead of him if he continues his journey towards Jerusalem. The Pharisees, Sadducees and Herodians who have been dogging his steps throughout his ministry will ensure that he is destroyed.

However, to be absolutely sure that his course of action is what God wants, Jesus travels to Mount Hermon to find solitude for prayer. For Jesus the priority is always to ensure that it is not his will, but God's will that is being done. Is it God's desire for him to travel to Jerusalem and face death? The answer in the form of the transfiguration is a resounding 'yes'. There appear before him Moses and Elijah: Moses the great law-giver who brought God's will to men and women, and Elijah the great prophet who interpreted God's will to men and women. Their appearance points the way for Jesus to go.

Although we have been having fun and have consulted our own Oracles, the very best way of finding out what we should do is to ask God in prayer. When we are open to God's suggestions we will be amazed at what happens. For God will answer us through the ordinary things of our life, and when our plans synchronize with God's plans anything can happen.

ASH WEDNESDAY

Lent is the time when we should rethink our lifestyles, so that our worship and our lifestyle reflect each other.

Joel 2.1–2, 12–17 or Isaiah 58.1–12
2 Corinthians 5.20b—6.10
Matthew 6.1–6, 16–21 or John 8.1–11

- A copy of the nun picture for each person.
- A very large copy of the nun picture.
- A small piece of card for each person.
- Scissors.
- Glue.
- Bibles: At least one for each group.

□ *Starter*

Create small groups of mixed ages. Invite each group to make Lenten nun cards copying the pattern below. To ensure speed photocopy the picture of the nun onto card for each person. Cut out the nun.

Then as a group read Isaiah 58.1–7 (or 1–12) together. If

children are present in the group, use a suitable children's Bible. Discuss the meaning of the passage, and how much of the prophet's accusations still apply today. Are there other suggestions one could add to the list, that might be more applicable today? Choose some of them, as appropriate, and write them as a reminder, on the back of the nun's legs and feet.

For example you might wish to use some of the following, although other examples may occur to you:

- Do not quarrel.
- Do not get angry.
- Give justice to all.
- Give freedom to all.
- Give to those in need.
- Share your food with the hungry.
- Give the homeless shelter.
- Make yourself available to your family.

☐ *Conclusion*

Before the service make a large nun, with very large legs and feet. Now ask the groups for some of the things they have written on their nun's legs, particularly for any ideas applicable to today. Then choose the most popular and write onto the back of the large nun's legs. Hang in church and turn up one leg (and pin back) each week in Lent to remind the congregation of what it is that God wants from his people. Be reminded that God does not want outward signs of fasting and humility, rather he wants his people to live out their lives in a true spirit of love.

☐ *Comment*

At the time the prophet Isaiah is writing many Jews carried out their religious observances faithfully. Moses had brought them God's law, and in response they endeavoured to obey all that he commanded. They would pray regularly and fast as the law required. The problem was that it did not seem to affect the way they lived their lives in any way. At the time Isaiah was writing there was great inequality between the rich and the poor; the good were often punished for crimes they had not committed; and society was affected by great divisions.

Isaiah therefore takes the people to task. It is no good praying and fasting, he says, if this has no effect upon a person's life. The two must go hand in hand. If the people are truly repentant for their sins, then they will make changes in their life. They will begin to care for the poor, they will feed the hungry, clothe the naked, and care for the oppressed. Only when repentance and a changed life go hand in hand will the relationship be put right with God.

Lent is the time when we should seek to bring our lifestyle and our worship into line with each other. Lent is the time to change the way we live.

THE FIRST SUNDAY OF LENT

We can learn to break the power of temptation by thinking of the good of others, and by trying to understand what God might want.

Genesis 2.15–17; 3.1–7
Romans 5.12–19
Matthew 4.1–11

- Large sheets of frieze paper.
- Coloured leaves.
- Glue.
- Picture of the heads of a man and a woman.
- Temptation Cards for all the congregation.
- Pencils or pens.

☐ *Starter*
Arrange for the prayer of confession in this service to be held after the sermon slot.

Create a huge 'Temptation Board'. Put up large sheets of paper (or use the back of a roll of wallpaper) to make a frieze. When it is completed the frieze will show Adam and Eve hiding in the garden. Create two heads, one male and one female and paste them onto the paper first. Before the service photocopy leaf shapes (see Appendix) onto coloured paper (yellow, red, green, and brown). Give everyone a number of the leaf-shaped pieces of paper. Invite everyone to think of the many things that tempt people. You might wish to hold a discussion first, or you could use newspapers and magazines to help with ideas. Encourage the congregation to think beyond the most obvious by reminding them of how secular we have become as a society; of the way that we desire instant gratification; and of how personal satisfaction is always considered acceptable before the community good. Alternatively encourage people to talk together in small groups.

Members of the congregation should write as many temptations as possible on the front of the leaves, with one temptation on each separate leaf. When finished they should be stuck onto the large frieze, with the temptations uppermost, and with the leaves overlapping. Some of the leaves need not be completely stuck down, so as to give a three-dimensional 'forest'. The faces of Adam and Eve should only partially be covered.

Allow people time to read the temptations, and arrange to use some of them in the prayers of confession.

 ☐ *Comment*

In our readings today we see two different kinds of temptation. In Genesis, Adam and Eve are tempted by the snake into eating the apple of the tree of the knowledge of good and evil, despite God's express wish that this should not happen, while in the Gospel reading we see Jesus being tempted by the devil.

As usual when Jesus wants guidance he finds time to go away to talk with God. On this occasion he goes into the desert, not the sandy wasteland of our imagination, but the rocky mountains perhaps between Judea and the Dead Sea. A more dreadful place can hardly be imagined.

Here Jesus prays and fasts, preparing himself for the job that he has to do. At the end, when he is weak and his resistance is at its lowest, the temptations occur. These are temptations aimed just at Jesus. They would hardly tempt you or me. For temptation always has the chance of succeeding. It is always a struggle to overcome temptation. Otherwise it wouldn't be tempting. In Jesus' case we must note that he overcomes the temptations by putting God first. He thinks of God and not himself. He does not dwell on his hunger or on the huge task that lies ahead of him; he thinks only of God. God, he says, should not be tempted!

If Adam and Eve had put God first they would have refrained from breaking his law. If we too can learn to stop thinking of ourselves and concentrate on what God wants then we too will overcome temptation.

☐ *Conclusion*
If you made the nun's card on Ash Wednesday, turn up one of her feet and observe the words written there.

Gather in small groups. Discuss those temptations that group members find most difficult to overcome. Then as a group write these onto cards, and create a very short prayer at the bottom. Encourage everyone to keep their Temptation Card with them during Lent, and to use the prayer when they feel tempted.

~ *Temptation Prayer* ~

THE SECOND SUNDAY OF LENT

We are called to go on a journey through Lent. It is a journey of faith, and we travel with God.

Genesis 12.1–4a
Romans 4.1–5, 13–17
John 3.1–17

- Group leaders.
- Tasks.

☐ *Starter*

Before the service appoint group leaders who can enable a group to work together. Give each leader the following instructions, dividing the destinations between them. It will not matter if there are multiple groups going to each place. Each should be between six and eight in number. Children can work together if desired.

- You are to leave home tomorrow as a group and travel by the cheapest means to:
  the Arctic
  the Antarctic
  Mount Everest.
- As a group decide what one question you want to ask about the trip.
- As a group decide what one luxury item you wish to take with you.
- As a group decide what you need to take with you.
- As a group decide what problems might occur on the journey.

In the week before the service, the leaders are to work out a possible route to their destination, bearing in mind price restrictions. It will be cheaper, for example, to go by coach or train than to fly, but it may not be cheaper to sail than to fly. Leaders are to guess, and need not get exact prices or times for the journey. Price restrictions do not mean that you have to be reduced to walking for hundreds of miles! The group leaders might wish to provide maps to show the group the route they suggest is taken for their journey.

Ask the leaders to keep the whole scenario to themselves for the week beforehand.

Divide the congregation into groups of between six and eight people. The leaders are to explain the scenario and show their planning for the journey. Allow time for all this to be understood before looking at the four tasks. Note that the tasks are to be decided *as a group*.

☐ *Conclusion*

Hear back from each group. Did any group feel inclined to say, 'We don't wish to go to . . .'? Were the problems considered to be great? What did the group think they would need to take with them, and what questions did they want to ask? (e.g. 'Why are we going to . . .?')

□ *Comment*

In the reading from Genesis 12, we see God calling Abram. Abram had first heard from God when he was in Ur (Genesis 7.2–4), but now the instructions come quite clearly. Abram is to leave his country, his family, and even his father's house. There is to be no looking back, he is simply to leave. And where is he to go? When we were thinking of travelling across the world, we knew where we were to go, and we had some idea of how to get there. But Abram is simply told to go to the land where God will lead him. He does not know where this will be. It might be anywhere in the world; it might take days, weeks, or years to get there; and he may have to overcome difficulties beyond his imagining.

Abram goes on his epic journey, leaving his known world for the unknown, because God wills it. He leaves everything for a reward that he is never to see. His name is to be great, and a great nation will come from him, but he will never live to see all this. He goes because he trusts God to lead him, and to be with him every step of the way.

During Lent we are on a journey, a much simpler one than that travelled by Abram. Our journey is taking us towards Easter. We have thought about the kind of Lent we wish to live, whether we shall give up certain things, or take on other challenges, but like Abram we now have to move on. God has called us, and he will be with us throughout our Lenten journey. We simply have to trust him and keep going.

THE THIRD SUNDAY OF LENT

We make the journey of our life in the company of God. He is there protecting us; nurturing us; and guiding us. Yet at the first hint of a problem we lose faith and blame God.

Exodus 17.1–7
Romans 5.1–11
John 4.5–42

- Group leaders.
- Large sheets of paper.
- Before the service create a large banner with the phrase 'Don't blame God, trust him!' The words need to be written

in very large bold letters. The width of the strokes should be at least 6 cm.
- Glue.
- 10-cm squares of tissue paper.

☐ *Starter*

Appoint leaders before the service. They need to be involved with one of the following areas (appropriate to your circumstances), and at least a couple of leaders may need to be flexible enough to help by covering more than one area.

- School
- Office work
- Leisure activities
- Home
- Factory work
- Farm work
- College/University
- Another

Each leader will need a placard announcing the activity they are concentrating on, and you may need more than one leader on any one subject, depending on the size of the congregation and their backgrounds. Aim to have about six to eight people in each group. Children may wish to stay together, or they could be in mixed groups with adults.

Invite everyone to join a group. They are to choose a group with which they are involved, e.g. a child might choose school, or a particular leisure activity.

The task of each group is to explore the times when they have blamed God or someone else, within the context of the employment or activity. Make a list on a large sheet of paper of what has gone wrong in the last five years. For example, a group of people involved with farming might want to make a list which includes:

- Prices dropping
- EU regulations
- Crop blight
- Crop failure
- Too much rain
- Too much sun
- Too much wind
- Animal sickness

☐ *Comment*

Continuing the theme of journeying from last week (if used), this time we are into the future. Abraham is dead, and his successors have new problems. The people of Israel are still journeying, having left Egypt to seek the land that God has promised them, but now under the leadership of Moses.

They leave the wilderness of Zin in the Sinai peninsula,* a desolate place even today, and move on to Rephidim, the present-day Wadi Refayid*. Here they find themselves in difficulties, for they cannot find water. Despite the time they have been with Moses, their immediate reaction is to blame him for dragging them into such a place where they are likely to die if water cannot be found soon.

However, not only do the people blame Moses, they use the circumstances to test God. If God is really with them, then he will save them by producing water from the desert. Perhaps they are tired of trekking all over the peninsula, but instead of trusting Moses and God, they blame both for the position they are in.

We too blame God when things go wrong, as we have already seen. We do not trust him to care for us, and the first problem on our journey of faith sees us moaning at God. We need to learn to stop complaining and put our faith in God. We are his people, and he will care for us as he did the Israelites. God *can* produce water from the rock!

☐   *Conclusion*

Give everyone in the congregation a square of tissue paper, and then invite them to tear off tiny pieces of the paper, scrunch it up, and stick it on the letters of the banner. Continue until all the letters are covered, and a three dimensional phrase appears. Hang the banner in church to remind everyone to trust in God.

* There is some dispute over these sites, but these are the usually accepted modern sites.

THE FOURTH SUNDAY OF LENT:
MOTHERING SUNDAY

We explore true love by looking at two Old Testament stories of women who gave away their greatest possessions.

Exodus 2.1–10 or 1 Samuel 1.20–28
2 Corinthians 1.3–7 or Colossians 3.12–17
Luke 2.33–35 or John 19.25b–27

- 2 or 3 speakers.

☐ *Starter*

Invite two or three people to talk to the congregation about something that is precious to them. Encourage them to take the precious object with them if possible, and to share special memories with the congregation.

Then invite everyone to talk to their neighbour about things that are very special to them. These might be objects that they possess now, or they may have been owned in the past.

☐ *Comment*

Today our lectionary gives us a choice of Old Testament readings. Both have something in common. In Exodus we have the story of Moses as a baby. The Israelites are oppressed by the Egyptians. There are so many of them that they are seen as a threat to the Egyptians, and as a consequence Pharaoh orders the killing of Israelite male babies.

Moses' mother manages to keep her baby away from Pharaoh's officers for three months, but is finally forced to give him away. She places her most precious possession, her baby, in a basket and trusts him to the River Nile. Perhaps he will have some chance of life on the river, because he will have no chance if Pharaoh finds him.

In the second Old Testament reading we have the story of Elkanah and his wife Hannah. After years of failing to have a child, while she is at the shrine at Shiloh, the priest Eli promises that she will have a child. In return she promises the child to God. He will be dedicated to God and will live his life in the shrine attending the priest. To be without a child in Israel was a terrible thing, yet after waiting for many years Hannah offers her beloved child to God's work.

We have thought about things that are precious to us, yet I wonder if they are as precious as a living human being. Both of these Old Testament stories are about women who give away their most precious possession – a child. In each case the child is to grow up to continue God's work. One is Moses who will lead the Israelites away from Egypt to the promised land and bring them God's law. The other is Samuel who will become one of God's greatest prophets.

☐ *Conclusion*

In pairs, think about people who have been special to you. It might be someone living or dead. Tell each other who has been special in your life.

☐ *Prayer*

Close with a few words of prayer thanking God for all those things and people that have been precious to us throughout our lives.

THE FIFTH SUNDAY OF LENT

If God can revive bones in the desert, he can revive his body the Church. We only need the faith to let him work in and through us.

Ezekiel 37.1–14
Romans 8.6–11
John 11.1–45

- Find someone to be 'Prophet Ex'.
- Someone to read the part of God.
- A group of the congregation to act out the reading.
- Copies of the Ezekiel 37 drama.

☐ *Starter*

Invite someone to act as an evangelist. Their name is 'Prophet Ex' Their task is to preach in an over-the-top evangelistic style. Introduce them in such a way that the congregation realize this is an act.

The evangelist should cover the following in a two-minute 'harangue':

- We are all sinners.
- We are all going to hell.
- However God can save us.

Intervene at this point to ask Prophet Ex what we can do to change. The evangelist then asks for as many people as possible to stand up. (You may need to prime some people beforehand and calm their fears about what is going to happen.) Tell them they are to become a living parable. They should listen to the words of the evangelist and carry out the actions he says. First they should find themselves some space in the church. They may sit, lie, or stand, but they need to be motionless. It would be helpful if they took up different positions. From now on the evangelist will organize a piece of drama based on Ezekiel 37. The 'actors' should remain absolutely still until the prophet indicates that they are to begin acting. God should be 'off stage' and out of sight.

Prophet Ex	The hand of the Lord came upon me, and he brought me out by the spirit of the Lord and set me down in the middle of a valley; it was full of bones. [*He waves his hand over the congregation standing.*] He led me all round them: [*walks around those standing*] there were very many lying in the valley, and they were very dry. God said to me,
God	Mortal, can these bones live?
Prophet Ex	I answered, 'O Lord God, you know.' Then he said to me,
God	Prophesy to these bones, and say to them: 'O dry bones, hear the word of the Lord. Thus says the Lord God to these bones: I will cause breath to enter you, and you shall live. I will lay sinews on you, and will cause flesh to come upon you, and cover you with skin, and put breath in you, and you shall live: and you shall know that I am the Lord.' So I prophesied as I had been commanded: and as I prophesied, suddenly there was a noise, a rattling, and the bones began to come together, bone to its bone. [*The Prophet indicates to the actors that they should now begin to move as appropriate.*] I looked and the toes began to wiggle . . . [*leave time for each action to occur*] the feet to rotate . . . the knees to bend . . . the legs to lift . . . bottoms to wiggle . . . stomachs to rotate . . . fingers to twitch . . . hands to shake . . . arms to raise . . . shoulders to lift . . . necks to rotate . . . heads to nod and shake . . . eyes to open and shut . . . noses to twitch . . . mouths to open . . .

	I looked and there were sinews on them, and flesh had come upon them, but there was no breath in them. Then God said to me,
God	Prophesy to the breath, prophesy, mortal, and say to the breath: 'Thus says the Lord God: Come from the four winds, O breath, and breathe upon these slain that they may live.'
Prophet Ex	I prophesied as he commanded me, and the breath came into them, and they lived, and stood on their feet, a vast multitude. [*Actors all stand.*] Then he said to me,
God	Mortal, these bones are the whole house of Israel. They say, 'Our bones are dried up, and our hope is lost; we are cut off completely.' Therefore prophesy, and say to them. 'Thus says the Lord God: I am going to open your graves, and bring you up from your graves, O my people; and I will bring you back to the land of Israel. And you shall know that I am the Lord, when I open your graves, and bring you up from your graves, O my people. I will put my spirit within you, and you shall live, and I will place you on your own soil; then you shall know that I, the Lord, have spoken and will act.'
Prophet Ex	And all the people jumped for joy and shouted: Hallelujah. [*Everyone shouts Hallelujah, and the actors jump while shouting Hallelujah.*]

□   *Comment*

The prophet Ezekiel was taken with King Jehoiachin and other important people of Judah into captivity to Babylon. They were obviously allowed some considerable freedom for they were free to worship and to build their own houses. However, despite the fact that Ezekiel is removed from Israel, the fate of his beloved country still concerns him, and in particular the fate of Jerusalem. Like his predecessors before him he prophesied doom. But unlike Jeremiah his prophecies also concern the whole state and all 'the house of Israel' whether they are living in Judah, Jerusalem or Babylon.

Ezekiel's prophecies were often accompanied by amazingly dramatic signs. So for instance he cut off his hair using a sword and divided it into three parts to show what would happen to the people of Israel. The people seemed slightly amused by his extravagant gestures, but they did not really take his prophecies to heart, until the city of Jerusalem fell. However, from now on Ezekiel's message begins to change to one of hope.

Ezekiel's wonderful image of the valley of dry bones is a vibrant message to the people of Israel. No doubt they thought of the many people who had been killed at the fall of Jerusalem and at the valley below the city where the dead were buried. Ezekiel is asked by God, 'Mortal, can these bones live?', and at God's command he prophesies to the bones. Suddenly the bones become living human beings, through the power of the Spirit.

Ezekiel's vision is about bringing Israel to life as one people, about Judah and Israel coming together again, but we can also apply it to ourselves today. God can create life out of dry bones; God can create life out of the dry bones of our lives and out of the dry bones of our church life. He can bring us back to full life.

☐ *Conclusion*

Hold a discussion about the drama with the whole congregation. Ask the following questions:

- How did you feel to be told by the evangelist, Prophet Ex, before the drama, that we are all sinners and will go to hell?
- Do you believe in a physical hell (on earth or beyond this world)?
- Ezekiel says that God can save his people by putting his Spirit into them? Do you believe he can?
- *(to the actors)* How did it feel to come alive after being 'dead bones'?
- If God can revive dead bones, then surely he can revive us as individuals, and he can revive us as a church, too. What do you feel about revival in your life and in this church? Where you do think it should start?

☐ *Prayer*

End with a short prayer asking for God's help to revive the faith of the congregation; to revive the work of the church; to revive the work of the leadership.

PALM SUNDAY

The passion of Jesus Christ is explored through drama involving all the congregation.

Isaiah 50.4–9a
Philippians 2.5–11
Matthew 26.14—27.66 (passion reading)

- Sufficient copies of the passion reading, below, for all the congregation.
- Appoint actors the week before if desired: see list below.
- Props: see list below.

□ *Starter*

Carry out some drama based on the full passion reading today. Before the service photocopy the reading, below, and plan an allocation of parts. Collect the various props needed. You might wish to give out parts the week before so that people can read through the script. Use the whole of the space in the church, and microphones if necessary for the main parts. Ensure that the parts of the narrators are carried out by good actors who are able to hold the action together. Give those with 'small voices' action parts, rather than large voice parts. If desired, actors could dress up.

All the congregation should be involved in the drama. Those who do not wish to participate in the acting can still read the parts. Younger children can join in with the crowd scenes and don't need to read the parts. With a large congregation have double parts, one to read and one to act.

Encourage everyone to really enter into the drama by a short rehearsal, as follows:

□ *Rehearsal*

Divide the actors into their various parts:

- Disciples and Jesus
- Pilate and his entourage/chief priests and other priests
- Crowd

Any parts not covered in the above (e.g. the two girls) can join the last group. Using three leaders, find a separate place in the church to run through some simple actions. The following scenes would be worth a short rehearsal. Do not worry too much about the words, but just walk through some of the movements, or crowd reactions that will be expected:

- last supper or garden of Gethsemane
- first scene with Pilate
- crowd reaction with Pilate and at the crucifixion

Only spend four or five minutes at maximum in rehearsal. Aim for dramatic effect and encourage the cast to *act* as feels appropriate.

THE PASSION READING

Actors

Narrator 1	Bystanders
Narrator 2	Girl 1
Chief priest	Girl 2
Priests	Pilate
Judas	Barabbas
Servant	Pilate's wife
Jesus	Pilate's servant
Disciples (minimum of 5)	Soldiers
Women and children	Simon
Peter	Two bandits
James	Mary, the mother of Jesus
John	Mary Magdalene
Crowd	Mary, the mother of James and John
Witnesses	Two other women
Slave	Joseph of Arimathea

Props

Bag of money
Trestle tables
Food, plates, etc. for last supper
Benches or chairs
Hymn words (optional)
Chalice, wine, paten, bread
2 swords
2 clubs (baseball or rounders bats!)
2 lots of rope
Gag
Bowl and towel
Whip (made from soft string)
Red cloak or red material
Crown of thorns (made from twigs)
Small stick
Dice
3 fairly large crosses and rope for each
Hammer(s) and nails (or imaginary)
Notice saying: 'This is Jesus, King of the Jews'
Sponge on a small stick
A white sheet

Narrator 1

Then one of the twelve, who was called Judas Iscariot, went to the chief priests and said,
[*The chief priest and a number of other priests stroll forward to a central point. Judas moves from the back, looking round furtively*]

Judas	[*bowing*] Sirs, what will you give me if I betray Jesus to you? [*The priests laugh at him and turn away*] Sirs, what will you give me? I *will* betray him to you. [*The chief priest calls a young servant to him to bring some money. The servant enters carrying a bag of money*]
Chief priest	Here are 30 pieces of silver. Make sure you do your work well. [*The priests exit, and Judas returns to the back of the church*]
Narrator 1	From that moment Judas began to look for an opportunity to betray Jesus.
Narrator 2	On the first day of the Feast of Unleavened Bread the disciples came to Jesus. [*Five or six disciples enter with Jesus, talking as they walk*]
Disciples	Where do you want us to make the preparations for you to eat the Passover?
Jesus	Go into the city to a certain man that I will tell you of, and say to him, 'The Teacher says, "My time is near: I will keep the Passover at your house with my disciples."' [*Four disciples exit the way they have come. Jesus and one other disciple exit the opposite way*]
Narrator 2	The disciples did as Jesus had directed them, and they prepared the Passover meal for him. [*The four disciples, along with some women or children, if desired, now bring in a trestle table and chairs and begin to set up the meal. Narrator 2 waits until preparations are almost ready before speaking. The disciples gather around the table and begin to 'eat and drink.' Judas is next to Jesus*]
Narrator 1	When it was evening, Jesus took his place with the twelve; and while they were eating, he said . . .
Jesus	Truly I tell you, one of you will betray me.
Narrator 1	The disciples were greatly distressed and began to say to him one after another . . .
Disciples	[*all together, but overlapping*] Surely not I, Lord?
Jesus	[*holding his hand up to stop the denials*] The one who has dipped his hand into the bowl with me will betray me.

	[*At that point it so happens that Judas who is sitting next to Jesus has his hand in a dish near Jesus. He removes his hand sharply and looks round furtively*] The Son of Man goes as it is written of him, but woe to that one by whom the Son of Man is betrayed! It would have been better for that one not to have been born. [*He looks at Judas*]
Narrator 1	Judas, who was to betray Jesus, said . . .
Judas	Surely it is not I, Rabbi?
Jesus	*You* have said so, Judas!
Narrator 1	While they were eating, Jesus took a loaf of bread, and after blessing it he broke it and gave it to his disciples, and said . . . [*Jesus picks up a small loaf of bread, holds it up high, then breaks it in half, and begins to pass large pieces of the bread to the disciples who are either side of him*]
Jesus	Take, eat; this is my body.
Narrator 1	Then he took a cup, and after giving thanks he gave it to them, saying . . . [*Jesus picks up a glass or chalice, holds it up, then passes it to a disciple*]
Jesus	Drink from it, all of you; for this is my blood of the covenant, which is poured out for many for the forgiveness of sins. I tell you, I will never again drink of this fruit of the vine until that day when I drink it new with you in my Father's kingdom. [*The disciples begin to clear away the meal, and a hymn can be sung, something that is known by heart, preferably*]
Narrator 1	When they had sung the hymn, they went out to the Mount of Olives. [*Jesus and the disciples begin to move away to another part of the church*] Then Jesus said to the disciples . . .
Jesus	You will all become deserters because of me this night: for it is written, 'I will strike the shepherd, and the sheep of the flock will be scattered.' But after I am raised up, I will go ahead of you to Galilee.
Narrator 1	Peter said to him . . .
Peter	[*firmly*] Though all become deserters because of you, I will never desert you.

Jesus	[*sadly*] Truly I tell you, this very night, before the cock crows, you will deny me three times.
Peter	[*vehemently*] Even though I must die with you, I will not deny you.
Narrator 1	And so said all the disciples. [*All the disciples reject Jesus' words*]
Narrator 2	Then Jesus went with them to a place called Gethsemane; [*Jesus and the disciples move off to another part of the church, perhaps towards the chancel steps. Peter picks up a sword and takes it with him*]
Jesus	Sit here while I go over there and pray. [*The disciples, except Peter, James and John, sit down, and gradually fall asleep*]
Narrator 2	He took with him Peter and James and John the sons of Zebedee, and he began to be grieved and agitated. Then he said to them . . . [*Jesus, Peter, James and John move a little away, perhaps towards the sanctuary*]
Jesus	I am deeply grieved, even to death; remain here, and stay awake with me. [*Peter, James and John sit down, and gradually fall asleep*]
Narrator 2	And going a little further, he threw himself on the ground and prayed. [*Jesus moves away, perhaps to the sanctuary, and falls onto his knees, in anguish*]
Jesus	My Father, if it is possible, let this cup pass from me; yet not what I want but what you want.
Narrator 2	Then Jesus came to the disciples and found them sleeping; and he said to Peter . . .
Jesus	Could you not stay awake with me one hour? Stay awake and pray that you may not come to the time of trial; [*shaking his head sadly*] the spirit indeed is willing, but the flesh is weak.
Narrator 2	Again he went away for a second time and prayed . . . [*Jesus returns to the sanctuary and kneeling down, prays, in anguish. The disciples try hard to keep awake and to pray, but gradually fall asleep again*]
Jesus	My Father, if this cannot pass unless I drink it, your will be done.

Narrator 2	Again he came and found the disciples sleeping, for their eyes were heavy. [*Jesus returns to the disciples, sees they are asleep and returns to the sanctuary, again to pray*] So leaving them again, he went away and prayed for the third time, saying the same words. [*Jesus prays in great anguish, again*] Then he came to the disciples and said to them . . . [*Jesus returns to the disciples, who wake up at his words*]
Jesus	Are you still sleeping and taking your rest? See the hour is at hand and the Son of Man is betrayed into the hands of sinners. Get up, let us be going. See, my betrayer is at hand. [*Jesus points to the back of the church where a crowd of people have appeared, headed by Judas Iscariot, the chief priest and other priests. The crowd move towards Jesus and the disciples as the Narrator speaks*]
Narrator 2	While he was still speaking, Judas, one of the Twelve, arrived; with him was a large crowd with swords and clubs, from the chief priests and the elders of the people. Now the betrayer had given them a sign, saying, 'The one I will kiss is the man: Arrest him.' At once, then, Judas came up to Jesus and said . . .
Judas	Greetings, Rabbi! [*Judas comes up to Jesus, and kisses him on both cheeks*]
Jesus	[*sadly*] Friend, do what you are here to do.
Narrator 2	Then they came and laid hands on Jesus and arrested him. [*The whole crowd descend on Jesus, pushing the disciples, except for Peter, out of the way*] Suddenly, one of those with Jesus put his hand on his sword, drew it, and struck the slave of the high priest, cutting off his ear. [*Peter picks up his sword and attacks the slave, who is endeavouring to manhandle Jesus. The slave holds his hand to his ear in agony. Jesus puts up his hand to stop Peter*]
Jesus	Put away your sword. Do you think that I cannot appeal to my Father, and he will at once send me more than 12 legions of

	angels? But how then would the scriptures be fulfilled, which say it must happen in this way?
Narrator 2	Then Jesus spoke to the crowd . . .
Jesus	Have you come out with swords and clubs to arrest me as though I were a bandit? Day after day I sat in the temple teaching, and you did not arrest me. But all this has taken place, so that the scriptures of the prophets may be fulfilled.
Narrator 2	Then all the disciples deserted him and fled. [*The disciples begin to slide away in different directions. Peter stays nearby, watching*] Those who had arrested Jesus took him to Caiaphas, the high priest, in whose house the scribes and the elders had gathered. But Peter was following him at a distance, as far as the courtyard of the high priest; and going inside, he sat with the guards in order to see how this would end. [*The crowd now manhandle Jesus away, to another part of the church, with Peter following*] Now the chief priests and the whole council were looking for false testimony against Jesus so that they might put him to death, but they found none, though many false witnesses came forward. [*A rough court is set up, with the chief priest seated centrally, and other priests surrounding him. Witnesses are called, who point aggressive fingers at Jesus. Finally two witnesses come forward together. Peter stays a way off, watching and warming himself at a fire with some bystanders*] At last two more witnesses came forward.
Witnesses	[*pointing to Jesus*] This fellow said, 'I am able to destroy the temple of God and to build it in three days.'
Narrator 2	The high priest stood up and said . . .
High priest	Have you no answer? What is it that they testify against you?
Narrator 2	But Jesus was silent. Then the high priest said to him . . .
High priest	I put you under oath before the living God, tell us if you are the Messiah, the Son of God.
Jesus	You have said so. But I tell you, from now on you will see the Son of Man seated at the

	right hand of power and coming on the clouds of heaven.
Narrator 2	Then the high priest tore his clothes and said . . .
High priest	[*standing, angry*] He has blasphemed! Why do we still need witnesses? You have now heard his blasphemy. What is your verdict?
Crowd	He deserves death! Kill him! [*The crowd now attack Jesus, hitting him, and spitting at him*] Prophesy to us, you Messiah! Who is it that struck you?
Narrator 1	Now Peter was sitting outside in the courtyard. A servant girl came to him and said . . . [*Enter Girl 1 to stand before Peter*]
Girl 1	You also were with Jesus the Galilean.
Narrator 2	But he denied it before all of them.
Peter	I do not know what you are talking about. [*Girl 1 exits*]
Narrator 2	When he went out to the porch, another servant girl saw him, and she said to the bystanders . . . [*Peter moves away slowly. Girl 2 enters to stand before him*]
Girl 2	[*talking to Peter and the others nearby*] This man was with Jesus of Nazareth.
Narrator 2	Again he denied it with an oath . . .
Peter	I do not know the man. [*Girl 2 exits. Those nearby begin to look more carefully at Peter*]
Narrator 2	After a little while some bystanders came up and said to Peter [*The bystanders come up to Peter*]
Bystanders	Certainly you are also one of them, for your accent betrays you. [*Peter begins to get angry*]
Narrator 2	Then Peter began to curse, and he swore an oath . . .
Peter	I do not know the man!
Narrator 2	Then Peter remembered what Jesus had said: 'Before the cock crows, you will deny me three times.' [*The crowing of a cockerel is heard, and Peter appalled begins to leave*] And he went out and wept bitterly.

Narrator 1	When morning came, the chief priest and the elders of the people conferred together against Jesus in order to bring about his death. They bound him, led him away, and handed him over to Pilate, the governor. [*Jesus is bound and the whole crowd take him to another part of the church. Pilate enters with some of his entourage in attendance. He remains at a distance during the next scene*] When Judas, his betrayer, saw that Jesus was already condemned, he repented and brought back the 30 pieces of silver to the chief priests and the elders. [*Judas comes forward and kneels before Pilate, but speaks to the chief priest*]
Judas	I have sinned by betraying innocent blood. Take this back.
Chief priest	[*waving him away*] What is that to me? See to it yourself.
Narrator 1	Throwing down the pieces of silver, he departed, and went out and hanged himself. [*Judas throws down the bag of money, and storms out to the back of the church*] But the chief priest, taking the pieces of silver, said . . . [*Chief priest picks up the bag of money*]
Chief priest	It is not lawful to put this into the treasury, since it is blood money.
Narrator 1	After conferring together, they used the money to buy the potter's field as a place to bury foreigners. For this reason that field has been called the Field of Blood to this day. Then was fulfilled what had been spoken through the prophet Jeremiah, 'And they took the thirty pieces of silver, the price of the one on whom some of the people of Israel had set a price, and they gave it for the potter's field, as the Lord had commanded.' [*The priests confer together, and the chief priest gives the money to one of them, who exits to buy the field*] Now Jesus stood before the governor. [*Pilate moves to centre, a chair is brought for him to sit on, and Jesus is pushed to stand before him*]
Pilate	Are you the King of the Jews?

Jesus	You say so.
Narrator 1	But when he was accused by the chief priest and elders, he did not answer.
Priests	He is guilty! [*the chief priest and elders, point accusingly at Jesus*]
	Then Pilate said to Jesus . . .
	[*The priests continue to say, 'He is guilty'*]
Pilate	Do you not hear how many accusations they make against you?
Narrator 1	But he gave him no answer, not even to a single charge, so that the governor was greatly amazed.
Narrator 2	Now at the festival the governor was accustomed to release a prisoner for the crowd, anyone whom they wanted. At that time they had a notorious prisoner, called Barabbas.
	[*A crowd of people enter bring the prisoner Barabbas, who is bound, to stand on the other side to Jesus, before Pilate*]
	So after they had gathered, Pilate said to them . . .
Pilate	Whom do you want me to release for you, Barabbas or Jesus who is called the Messiah?
Narrator 2	For he realized that it was out of jealousy that they had handed him over. While he was sitting on the judgement seat, his wife came bringing word to him . . .
	[*Enter Pilate's wife to speak to him. She stands behind him, and speaks quietly into his ear*]
Pilate's wife	Have nothing to do with that innocent man, for today I have suffered a great deal because of a dream about him.
	[*Pilate's wife stays behind Pilate*]
Narrator 2	Now the chief priest and the elders persuaded the crowds to ask for Barabbas and to have Jesus killed.
	[*The high priest and priests begin to stir up the people against Jesus*]
Priests	[*pointing to Jesus*] Kill him! He is guilty! He blasphemes.
Narrator 2	The governor again said to them . . .
Pilate	Which of the two do you want me to release for you?
Priests & crowd	Barabbas!

	[*Some keep on calling for Barabbas throughout this section*]
Pilate	Then what should I do with Jesus who is called the Messiah?
Priests & crowd	[*angry*] Let him be crucified!
	[*Some keep on calling for Jesus to be crucified*]
Pilate	Why, what evil has he done?
Narrator 2	But they shouted all the more . . .
Priests & crowd	[*angry*] Let him be crucified!
Narrator 2	So when Pilate saw that he could do nothing, but rather that a riot was beginning, he took some water and washed his hands before the crowd.
	[*Pilate claps his hands, and a servant enters carrying a bowl, with a towel over his arm*]
Pilate	I am innocent of this man's blood; see to it yourselves.
Narrator 2	Then the people as a whole answered . . .
Priests & crowd	His blood be on us and on our children!
Narrator 2	So he released Barabbas for them; and after flogging Jesus, he handed him over to be crucified.
	[*Pilate claps his hands and in come some soldiers. Jesus is held by two of them, as Jesus is whipped. Then they lead Jesus away, followed by the chief priest, the priests, and the crowd to the back of the church. Pilate, his wife, and his servant exit elsewhere*]
	The soldiers of the governor took Jesus into the governor's headquarters, and they gathered the whole cohort around him. They stripped him and put a scarlet robe on him, and after twisting some thorns into a crown, they put it on his head. They put a reed in his right hand and knelt before him and mocked him.
	[*The soldiers place a red cloak or piece of material on Jesus, a crown of thorns on his head, and a small stick into his right hand, before beginning to mock him. The crowd engage in general mockery also, bowing before him, etc.*]
All	Hail, King of the Jews.
Narrator 2	They spat on him, and took the reed and struck him on the head. After mocking him, they stripped him of the cloak and put his own clothes on him. Then they led him away to crucify him.

	[*The stick and cloak are taken away, and he is generally abused. A cross is brought in and Jesus is constrained to carry it. The whole crowd then begin to lead him back to the central point of the church*]
Narrator 1	As they went out, they came upon a man from Cyrene named Simon; they compelled this man to carry his cross.
	[*Simon enters and tries to pass through the crowd, but is forced to help Jesus carry the cross*]
	And when they came to a place called Golgotha (which means Place of a Skull), they offered him wine to drink, mixed with gall; but when he tasted it, he would not drink it. And when they had crucified him, they divided his clothes among themselves by casting lots; then they sat down there and kept watch over him. Over his head they put the charge against him, which read: 'This is Jesus, King of the Jews.'
	[*Some of the crowd exit to fetch the two bandits who enter a little later. A member of the crowd offers Jesus a bottle of wine. Jesus tastes it but then pushes it away. He is then tied onto the cross, with pretend nails being hammered into his hands and feet. The cross and Jesus are then stood up. The guards begin to play with dice, to decide who will get the cloak. One of the crowd places a notice over Jesus, saying, 'This is Jesus, King of the Jews'. Alternatively Jesus could hold the notice*]
Narrator 2	Then two bandits were crucified with him, one on his right and one on his left.
	[*Two bandits and brought in by members of the crowd. They carry a cross each, and are tied onto it, before they stand upright with their cross, either side of Jesus*]
	Those who passed by derided Jesus, shaking their heads . . .
Crowd	You who would destroy the temple and build it in three days, save yourself! If you are the Son of God, come down from the cross.
	[*Some of the crowd go up to him and mock him*]
Narrator 2	In the same way the chief priest also, along with the scribes and elders, mocked him.
	[*The priests also mock him*]
Chief priest & priests	He saved others; he cannot save himself. If he is the King of Israel let him come down

	from the cross now, and we will believe in him. He trusts in God; let God deliver him now, if he wants to; for he said, 'I am God's Son.'
Narrator 2	The bandits who were crucified with him also taunted him in the same way.
Narrator 1	From noon on, darkness came over the whole land until three in the afternoon. And about three o'clock Jesus cried with a loud voice . . .
Jesus	Eli, Eli, lema sabachthani?
	[*Jesus looks upwards*]
Narrator 1	That is, 'My God, my God, why have you forsaken me?'
	When some of the bystanders heard it, they said . . .
	[*The bystanders move forward towards Jesus, looking at him*]
Bystanders	This man is calling for Elijah.
Narrator 1	At once one of them ran and got a sponge, filled it with sour wine, put it onto a stick, and gave it to him to drink.
	[*One of the bystanders fetches a stick with a small sponge attached to the end of it, and offers it to Jesus*]
	But the others said . . .
Bystanders	Wait, let us see whether Elijah will come to save him.
	[*All move slightly away from Jesus now, leaving only one or two soldiers nearby, on duty*]
Narrator 1	Then Jesus cried again with a loud voice and breathed his last.
	[*Jesus cries aloud, and dies, his head falling downwards*]
	[*Pause, all remain in frozen position*]
	At that moment the curtain wall of the temple was torn in two, from top to bottom. The earth shook, and the rocks were split. The tombs also were opened, and many bodies of the saints who had died were raised. After his resurrection they came out of the tombs and entered the holy city and appeared to many. Now when the centurion and those with him, who were keeping watch over Jesus, saw the earthquake and what took place they were terrified and said . . .

	[*Soldiers move, reacting to what has happened. Other members of the cast remain frozen in position*]
Soldiers	Truly this man was God's Son!
	[*All the cast continue in frozen positions*]
Narrator 1	Many women were also there, looking on from a distance.
	[*Enter a number of women, including Mary, the mother of Jesus, and Mary Magdalene*]
	They had followed Jesus from Galilee and had provided for him. Among them were Mary Magdalene, and Mary the mother of James and Joseph, and the mother of the sons of Zebedee.
	[*The women move towards the cross, in great distress. Once in position they freeze*]
	When it was evening, there came a rich man from Arimathea, named Joseph who was also a disciple of Jesus.
	[*Enter Joseph from the back, to one side. Pilate appears with some of his entourage*]
	He went to Pilate . . .
Joseph	Give me the body of my master Jesus, I beg you, that I may bury him.
Pilate	[*claps his hands for a servant to appear*] Give the body of the Nazarite to this man. See to it.
	[*Pilate and his entourage exit. Joseph goes with the servant to where Jesus is. The body of Jesus is taken off the cross by the soldiers and he is 'led' away by Joseph, and the women. The soldiers and all other actors exit.*]
Narrator 1	So Joseph took the body and wrapped it in a clean linen cloth and laid it in his own new tomb, which he had hewn in the rock.
	[*A sheet is placed around Jesus and he is laid on the ground. All leave him in the tomb, to sit in vigil outside the tomb*]
	He then rolled a great stone in front of the door of the tomb and went away. Mary Magdalene and the other Mary were there, sitting opposite the tomb.
	[*pause*]
Narrator 2	The next day, that is, after the day of preparation, the chief priest and the Pharisees gathered before Pilate and said . . .
	[*Jesus, and the two Marys stay where they are*]

	[*Enter Pilate with his entourage, also the chief priest and the other priests*]
Chief priest	Sir, we remember what that impostor said while he was still alive, 'After three days I will rise again.' Therefore command that the tomb be made secure until the third day; otherwise his disciples may go and steal him away, and tell the people, 'He has been raised from the dead', and the last deception would be worse than the first.
Pilate	You have a guard of soldiers; go, make it as secure as you can.
	[*Exit Pilate and his entourage*]
Narrator 2	So they went with the guard and made the tomb secure by sealing the stone.
	[*The chief priest and other priests go to the tomb, where they stand either side of Jesus as guards. All freeze*]

There is no Conclusion or Comment this week.

MAUNDY THURSDAY

Jesus shows us what true humility is by washing the feet of his disciples, and by offering up his life for us.

Exodus 12.1–4 (5–10), 11–14
1 Corinthians 11.23–26
John 13.1–17, 31b–35

- Bowl.
- Water.
- Ewer or jug.
- Towel.
- OHP or flip chart and pens.
- Commitment forms for all the congregation.
- Pens or pencils.

☐ *Starter*

Before the service arrange to carry out some footwashing. This could be the feet of a number of the congregation, or of one person only. Jesus, the Son of God, the Messiah, washed the feet of ordinary Galileans. Make sure that your congregation reflect, if possible, something of the same dichotomy, e.g. a venerable, respected, businessman washing the feet of a teenager.

If possible, ensure that both the person washing the feet and the one whose feet are washed are not particularly keen to engage in the activity. When the footwashing is finished, ask those who have taken part to stay where they are.

Now read the Gospel at this point.

At the end of the reading begin to explore what it felt like to wash someone's feet, or to have your feet washed. The person asking the questions should not be the one who washed feet or had their feet washed.

You might want to ask some of the following questions:

- What did you think/feel when you were asked to wash someone's feet/or to have your feet washed?
- How did it feel to wash someone's feet/have your feet washed?
- What did you like or not like about the experience?

Do not be surprised if you receive secular and Christian responses.

Now enlarge the conversation to explore that 'first' footwashing of Jesus and the disciples. Invite the congregation to turn to their neighbour, and put the following questions up on an OHP or flip chart:

- Feet were always washed by slaves. How might the disciples have felt when Jesus washed their feet?
- Why do you think Jesus wanted to wash the disciples' feet?

☐ *Comment*

The hour of triumph was shortly to be here. Jesus knowing all things; knowing what lay ahead; and knowing that he had all power, washed his disciples' feet. He humbled himself to carry out the most demeaning of tasks. On the hot, dusty roads of Palestine feet became very dirty, and one of the first jobs of a host was to ensure that the visitor's feet were washed. Normally this would be the task of a slave or servant.

Sometimes we think ourselves too big to do the most menial of tasks. There is the businessman or woman who cannot make the tea or coffee in the office; there is the man or woman who cannot work at a local hostel for the homeless; there is the child who cannot play with a younger sibling. Yet when we love someone we can do the most humble of tasks. We can wash and clean a loved one when they are ill, we can get down on our hands and knees and clean up the mess caused by a loved one, we can descend to the level of a small child when we love them.

Jesus knew that he was about to be betrayed and rejected by his disciples. He might have been tempted to become bitter or cynical, but the reality is that the more he is hurt the more he loves humanity. God, he says, so loved the world that he sent his only Son into the world to save the world.

☐ *Conclusion*

Invite the congregation to work together in twos, to decide what one thing they could do that would be the equivalent of 'washing feet' for another human being in their life.

Before the service produce some 'commitment' forms on the following lines, and give each person a copy of the form and a pen or pencil:

~ *My foot-washing commitment* ~

I promise to

| by | date |

GOOD FRIDAY

Good Friday gives us the opportunity to meditate on all that Jesus did for us this day.

Isaiah 52.13—53.12
Hebrews 10.16–25 or Hebrews 4.14–16; 5.7–9
John 18.1—19.42

- A number of focal points, see below.
- Sheets of paper.
- Pencils or pens.
- Small flat candles.
- Tapers.
- Matches.

□ *Starter*

Before the service create focal points representing the events of Holy Week, for example:

- A large cross, a crown of thorns, and a red cloak or piece of material.
- Some large nails, a hammer, and a spear.
- A pottery chalice and paten, with bread and wine.
- A bowl, jug of water and a towel.
- A large crucifix or picture of the crucifixion.

There can be as many doubles of the above scenes as desired. If the congregation is liable to be large quite a few focal points will be needed. Invite as many creative people as possible to help with forming these focal points.

Beside each point put sheets of paper and pens or pencils.

Invite the congregation to start by looking at all the focal points. This should be done in silence. When they have looked at all of them go back to one point that 'speaks' to them. Pick up a piece of paper and a pencil or pen and then find somewhere to stand or sit where you can see the display. In silence write down all the words that come into your mind as a result of looking at the display. What does this say to you? If desired create a meditation or a poem. The work will be kept private.

□ *Comment*
The Good Friday story is one that we know so well that we can even begin to take it for granted. Then there are those people to whom the life of Jesus is so important that they cannot face the thought of his death. They avoid the Good Friday services like the plague and will not think about what happened to him.

All these people miss the point entirely. The story must never become so familiar that we lose the meaning and forget the dreadful death that took place on that day. It was not an unusual death at that time in the Roman empire for we know that just three years before the death of Jesus hundreds of people were crucified after a rebellion had taken place against the Roman authorities. But this death was different, for it happened to a man who committed no crime and whom we believe to be the Son of God. This fact alone should help us to keep the story real and alive in our minds.

But those who cannot face the reality of the death are equally wrong, for they need to remember every awful action of Jesus' death, before putting it in place as only a part of that weekend. The story does not end with the death of Jesus, if it did there would be no church and we would not be here. For that death was turned into triumph on the Sunday when Jesus broke the bounds of death and rose to life. We are the Easter people and our great message of hope rests on the resurrection and not on the death of Christ.

□ *Conclusion*
Give everyone a small candle (of the variety that can be set down on the floor or on the altar). Invite the congregation to place the candles on the floor in the shape of a cross, or alternatively on the altar (not in the shape of a cross). When everyone has returned to their seats ask one or two people to light the candles. Ensure that tapers are used and that the candles are lit by people not wearing robes (for safety reasons). Have a fire extinguisher handy.

□ *Optional*
Gather up the meditations in a bowl and offer to God. Burn afterwards.

EASTER DAY

As Christians we are 'Easter people'. Our faith is based not on the birth of Jesus, but on his resurrection.

Jeremiah 31.1–6
Colossians 3.1–4 or Acts 10.34–43
John 20.1–18 or Matthew 28.1–10

- 1 Easter Day Story sheet for each group.
- New Testament or Bible for each group.
- Pens or pencils.
- OHP, flip chart or frieze paper.
- OHP pen or fat pen.
- A3 sheets, glue, coloured pencils, white paper and scissors for each group.
- Pritt-Tak or pins to hang work.

☐ *Starter*
Before the service prepare a form, as shown below.

Divide the congregation into small groups of four to six people. Give each group a copy of the New Testament or a Bible, and allocate one of the four Gospels to each group. Also give each group an 'Easter Day Story' sheet and a pen or pencil. There can be as many groups as desired, as long as all four Gospels are covered.

Ask the groups to read the story of Easter *day* (i.e. morning, afternoon and evening) in the Gospel they have been allocated, and then jot down the events of the day on the Easter Day Story sheet.

As the first groups finish, transfer the information to an OHP or flip chart, or frieze paper, but keep this hidden from the congregation for the time being:

Easter Day Story

MATTHEW
Mary Magdalene & Mary
to tomb

MARK
Mary Magdalene, Mary mother
of James, & Salome took
spices to the tomb

LUKE
Women took spices to
the tomb

JOHN
Mary Magdalene to tomb

As the groups finish their task give them a sheet of A3 paper, pens, coloured pencils, scissors, glue, and paper. Their task is to create the first page of a newspaper describing the events of Easter Day as told only in their Gospel. They can use text, story, picture, or poetry to create the first page of their newspaper.

□   *Conclusion*

Spend some time looking at the different front pages, and compare the differences between the accounts of Easter Day which were produced earlier. Lastly, decide what the four accounts have in common.

□   *Comment*

We have four different accounts of Easter Day in the Gospels of Matthew, Mark, Luke and John. Most of the material in our Gospels, however, existed in oral form for very many years before it was transferred to the written word sometime between AD 60 and 100. During these first years the stories and information were gradually collected together before being put down on paper. Perhaps it is amazing that the stories are so very similar. If we were asked to recount what happened here today our accounts would surely differ, even though we might be writing them down just half an hour after the experience.

What is amazing is the amount of similarity between the stories, recorded by many different people, years later. All of them recount that the women came to the tomb the next morning, all agree that an angel or a man or men met them. Three of these sent the disciples to Galilee where they would meet Jesus.

As Christians we are an Easter People. Our faith is based on the events of Easter, and not on the events of Christmas, as odd as that might seem. For the Son of God to be born was amazing, but if that was all that happened the story would probably end there. It is Easter that makes this story so astounding. For we worship a God whose Son overcame death and who rose again to take our sins upon his shoulders.

THE SECOND SUNDAY OF EASTER

As Christians we are called not just to come *in* to church to worship. We are also called to go *out* into the world to do God's work.

Exodus 14.10–31; 15.20–21
1 Peter 1.3–9 or Acts 2.14a, 22–32
John 20.19–31

- OHP, transparencies of St James' Church, or outlines drawn on cardboard and a board and pins.
- Words of the rhyme for everyone.
- Large sheets of paper attached to the walls.
- Pens or pencils for everyone.

☐ *Starter*

Create 'St James' Church' by making a model of the church. Before the service get an 'artist' to draw up the outlines for all the physical parts of the church that you will need. These should be drawn onto thin card and can then be pinned onto a board. Alternatively draw the outlines onto OHP transparencies and overlay these onto one another. The following will be needed:

- Walls made of stone blocks (to cover three side of a rectangle, i.e. for three sides to allow us to look in through one side wall into the church).
- A roof made of wooden beams and slates (but only one side actually covered, to allow us to see inside).
- A steeple to stand at the end of the church (one side open to allow us to see inside).
- A bell in the open side of the steeple.
- A door, half open to add into one wall.
- Pews to put inside the church.
- People to put into the church.

You will need to produce the words of the rhyme for all to read together. As the rhyme is read add the overlays on the OHP, or put up the different parts of the model.

ST JAMES' CHURCH

This is the church
    that James built.
These are the stones *(add wall)*
    that support the church
    that James built.
This is the roof *(add roof)*
    that keeps out the rain,
    that's held up by the stones
    that support the church
    that James built.
This is the steeple *(add steeple)*
    that adjoins the roof
    that keeps out the rain,
    that's held up by the stones
    that support the church
    that James built.
This is the bell *(add bell)*
    that calls the people to worship,
    that hangs in the steeple
    that adjoins the roof
    that keeps out the rain,
    that's held up by the stones

that support the church
that James built.
This is the door *(add door)*
    that welcomes the people
    that are called by the bell to worship,
    that hangs in the steeple
    that adjoins the roof
    that keeps out the rain,
    that's held up by the stones
    that support the church
    that James built.
These are the pews *(add pews)*
    that seat the people
    that come through the door
    that are called by the bell to worship,
    that hangs in the steeple
    that adjoins the roof
    that keeps out the rain,
    that's held up by the stones
    that support the church
    that James built.
These are the Christians *(add people)*
    who sit on the pews,
    that come through the door
    that are called by the bell to worship,
    that hangs in the steeple
    that adjoins the roof
    that keeps out the rain,
    that's held up by the stones
    that support the church
    that James built.

 ☐ *Comment*

The disciples meet together, perhaps in the upper room where they had held the last supper, after the remarkable events of that Easter morning. They are scared. Will they be the next to lose their lives now that the religious authorities have taken Jesus' life? Will they be hunted down and killed? So the doors are locked.

But locked doors hold no problems for the risen Christ. Suddenly he is there among them. He shows them his hands with the tell-tale marks of his crucifixion. He greets them in his normal calm fashion, 'Peace be with you!' They have scarcely taken in his appearance, when they are given the first of a number of remarkable commands. There is no time for niceties, it is time to be moving.

Jesus says to them, 'As the Father has sent me, so I send you.' They are to be sent forth to do God's work. Jesus has completed his task, he has made it possible for his disciples to continue with his Father's work. Now he will be with them always. Through him they receive the power to do God's work. Here are the first priests being sent forth, out into the world to continue the work that Jesus started. But here too are the first Christians being sent forth out into the world.

☐ *Conclusion*

Before the service put up a number of large sheets of paper around the church, with the following headings: Church committee; Children; Teenagers; Leaders/Ministers; Church building; Social committee; Women's Group/Mothers' Union. (Add other headings as appropriate to your church.) Give everyone a pen or pencil (fat pens would be preferable).

Now look again at the model church 'that James built', which you have created. Suggest that there is something essentially wrong with this church and there is perhaps also something wrong with our church.

> The rhyme ends with this verse:
> These are the Christians
> who sit on the pews,
> that come through the door
> that are called by the bell to worship . . .

Comment that everything about the rhyme is concerned with bringing people into church to worship. However, Jesus' words to his disciples are about going *out* to take the message of God to the world, not of bringing people *in* to worship.

Invite everyone to turn to their neighbour and discuss how any of the groups in their church might change what they do so that they 'look outward' and not 'inward'. When they have made some decisions they should go and write up their comments onto one of the sheets.

THE THIRD SUNDAY OF EASTER

We are called to listen to God's word, to learn more about him, and then to tell others, as evangelists.

Zephaniah 3.14–20
1 Peter 1.17–23 or Acts 2.14a, 36–41
Luke 24.13–35

> - Copies of the Bible references for each group.
> - Bibles or New Testaments for everyone, if possible.
> - Pieces of paper and a pen or pencil for each group.
> - Large board headed 'Evangelism is telling the story'.
> - Pins to attach the paper to the board.

☐ *Comment*

The account of the journey to Emmaus is found in St Luke's Gospel. We do not know now where the village of Emmaus is although Luke says it is about seven miles from Jerusalem. Several places have been suggested, but none has been proved to be correct. Nevertheless this is one of the most important stories in the Gospel. It is a parable of how the Christian faith should be lived.

First, we see the two disciples returning to Emmaus after the dreadful events in Jerusalem two days before. They are wretchedly dejected because their Lord, the one they believed to be the Messiah, has been killed. Suddenly they are joined by a stranger who travels along with them, seemingly not knowing what has happened. His ignorance leads the two disciples to explain about Jesus, about their hopes for him, about the dreadful events surrounding his death, and the amazing news that the women did not find his body in the tomb when they went to it this morning.

In response to their words the stranger begins to teach the two men about God's purpose for the world and for his people. The two men are keen to continue listening to him and invite him into the house for the night. But it is only over the meal (which must surely stand for the Eucharist/communion service) that the men recognize their guest to be Jesus himself. Even as they recognize him, however, he disappears. Their immediate response is to return to Jerusalem to tell the others their news.

We are like the two men on the road to Emmaus. We are called to tell others (to be evangelists!) about Jesus and about

God's plan for the world, and in turn we are called to listen and learn. It is in the Eucharist that we meet and recognize the living Lord, our Saviour, Jesus Christ, and this in turn strengthens us to go out into the world to be evangelists, to tell others of our experience.

☐ *Starter*

Divide the congregation into small groups of between four and six people. Give each group a number of Bibles or New Testaments. The *group's* task is to find a story from the Bible that appeals to them, and then to decide what is its essential message. In other words, they are to decide what it can teach them. It would be helpful if the group could jot down the Bible reference and some notes on what the story has to say to them.

The groups might like to find their own stories, but it might be preferable to give them a list, which includes less well-known stories. Encourage the groups to look at a number of stories before settling on one.

☐ *Bible stories*

John 5.2–9 (or 15)
John 6.22–27a (or 35)
John 6.47–58
John 10.1–6 (or 7–18)
John 15.1–8
Acts 3.1–10
Acts 5.1–11
Acts 8.9–24
Acts 9.10–22
Acts 10.1–15 (or 48)
Acts 13.1–5a
Acts 16.11–15
Acts 17.15–28 (or 34)
Acts 18.1–11
Acts 18.24–28
Acts 20.7–12

Finally when the group has chosen the story that they feel speaks to them, and have decided what message it has for us today, they are to send one or two people on to another group (as evangelists!). Here the evangelists are to tell their story to the new group in their own words, and then expound the message it has for us today.

Ensure that all groups send one or two people out as evangelists, and every group receives one or two people as evangelists. This can be repeated a number of times, as time allows.

□ *Conclusion*

Before the service create a large board headed 'Evangelism is telling the story'. Encourage all the groups to pin their Bible references and notes onto this board to remind everyone that they are all evangelists.

THE FOURTH SUNDAY OF EASTER

Jesus the Good Shepherd cares for his sheep. We are the sheep and he is our shepherd.

Genesis 7
1 Peter 2.19–25 or Acts 2.42–47
John 10.1–10

- Shepherd (and sheep) or farmer, or alternatively a primed speaker.
- Interviewer.
- Second speaker to talk about sheep in Palestine.
- OHP or flip chart and tables.
- OHP pens or fat pens.

□ *Starter*

Invite a shepherd (and sheep if possible) to come into church (or the churchyard) to talk about sheep generally. An urban church might still try to find an ex-farmer who knows something about sheep.

Ask the farmer to look at some of the following:

- Sheep habits: Do they follow each other, do they try to escape, etc?
- Sheep ailments
- Sheep enemies
- Problems farming with sheep today: prices and costs, etc.

If a farmer cannot be found, the following information might be useful to conduct an interview with a fictional farmer.

SHEEP

Sickness

- When sick, sheep stand with their heads down, ears flat, eyes sad, and they walk badly.
- Sheep are prone to problems with their feet and skin; parasite worms in the stomach; and they attract flies which lay their eggs in cuts or abrasions, thus the sheep begin to breed maggots.
- The most dangerous illness is sheep scab which is a notifiable illness causing flocks to be destroyed.

Prevention

- Sheep are dipped in July, as the hot weather comes in, against fly maggots, and again in the autumn against sheep scab.

Breeding

- Sheep breed earlier and earlier. Their breeding cycle is governed by the length of the day – the shorter the day, the more virile they become.
- Many lambs are now born before Christmas.
- Normally lambs are born as the grass begins to grow – in March.
- Gestation period is 21 weeks.
- Between 50% and 60% of ewes in a flock will have twins, and about 10% triplets.
- Approximately 10% of a flock is kept for breeding and the rest is sold for slaughter or breeding.
- Wool is almost worthless. Australia, for instance, has approximately 20 years of global stock.

Food

- Sheep eat fresh grass, dried grass, hay, straw and concentrated corn with added minerals.

(From *The Sermon Slot* by Sharon Swain, SPCK 1993.)

Now turn to look at the traditions of sheep farming in Israel some 2,000 years ago, comparing the modern day with the past. Use another speaker, and if desired follow the same format of the interview. The following information might be useful.

THE SHEPHERD IN PALESTINE

- The shepherd had a hard life. He spent all his time caring for the sheep. They were never left alone. He found them fresh pasture and water, and he kept them safe, rescuing them from steep crags and dangerous ravines as well as natural predators like the wolf.
- At night, on the hills, the shepherd protected the sheep by placing them in circular pens built out of local stone. The entrance would be open, and the shepherd would lie down in the open doorway to keep the sheep in and the wolves out. He protected the sheep with his body.
- In the village sheep were collected together communally and protected by one man who kept the key to the door. Only a legitimate shepherd could lead his flock from here.
- The work of a shepherd was lonely as he was often away for months at a time searching for the freshest grass in the mountains and hills.
- The shepherd endured cold since the temperature at night in the mountains often falls below freezing.
- The shepherd's life was a dangerous one, for as well as wolves there were snakes, scorpions and even robbers with which to contend. He would also be forced to climb dangerous places to search among the crags and cliffs for lost sheep.
- In Palestine sheep were kept for wool, so over the years they got to know the shepherd and his voice.

☐ *Comment*

Jesus tells his listeners that he is the Good Shepherd. Sheep were so prevalent in Palestine that everyone would know what he meant by a 'good shepherd'. They could see the evidence of bad shepherds, who let their flocks wander and get into danger. The good shepherd did all he could to protect his flock, even to the extent of giving up his own life.

Jesus is the Good Shepherd, and we are his flock. He leads us to fresh pastures, he guides us in safe ways, and he protects us from danger. As we get to know him we recognize his voice; we recognize his involvement in our lives; and we put more trust in him.

The image is not so common to us today, for we are not normally surrounded by sheep and we do not know their habits and customs. For the first-century Jew there was no more common experience. Perhaps today the image of a good parent (or carer) would be more suitable. The good parent does all they can for their child. They love them, nurture them, and protect them – with their own life, if necessary. Equally, we have all seen what a bad parent is like and can make comparisons between the two.

A Good Shepherd   A Good Parent

Protects sheep from wolves, robbers etc.

Finds them new pasture etc.

Protects children from fire, cold, heat, other people etc.

~ Jesus, our Good Shepherd ~

Protects us from Satan

Feeds us spiritual food

....

....

☐ *Conclusion*

Using an OHP or flip chart write up the table shown in the illustration.

Encourage the congregation to fill in the two columns on the table, showing the characteristics of a good shepherd and a good parent. The latter may have a much longer list!

Finally on another sheet or transparency look at what Jesus does for us as our Good Shepherd. Look up the characteristics of the Good Shepherd and then apply them to ourselves. Write up the table in the illustration.

THE FIFTH SUNDAY OF EASTER

The church of God rests on Christ as the foundation stone. It also rests on those Christians who have gone before us.

Genesis 8.1–19
1 Peter 2.2–10 or Acts 7.55–60
John 14.1–14

- 30–40 cardboard boxes of all sizes.
- Sufficient A4 sheets of 'bricks' for everyone in the congregation.
- A4 sheets of 'bricks' with the names of patriarchs, prophets and saints written on them.
- A large amount of glue.
- Hymn words.

☐ *Starter*

Before the service collect as many cardboard boxes as possible. They can be all sizes and shapes. You will need at least 30–40 boxes, and a large space in which to work. You may find it easier to work outside.

Invite some of the congregation to come and help you build a church from the boxes. They are to create a three-dimensional building, with windows and a door (optional tower). They can take instructions from the congregation, or they can ignore them, as they please. Allow some time for this to happen.

Finally when the builders have finished admire their work or commiserate if they have found it impossible to put in doors and windows. Then ask them to sit down.

☐ *Comment*

The New Testament reading from 1 Peter 2.2–10 speaks of Jesus as the corner stone of a house, that is the stone that keeps the whole house together. It is the foundation stone. Without the foundation stone the house is not stable and the other stones will eventually fall down.

Peter is talking not just about a house, he is of course talking about the church, that is the people of God. Discuss the two different meanings of church, as the building, and as the people of God, if desired. Peter imagines them like a house, built on Jesus, the foundation stone. In other words we are to be living stones, creating a strong community, all resting on Jesus.

However, the present-day church doesn't just rest on Jesus. Before us there have been hundreds of thousands of Christians, all helping in their way to build a strong church. We are but a part of the church. We are the living church, if you like, but the whole church is comprised of those who have died and who are now with God, and with those to come. All of us make up the church of God.

☐ *Conclusion*

Before the service prepare sheets of A4 paper (or smaller depending on the size of the congregation and the size of the cardboard church) with a brick shape drawn on them. Also prepare some brick shapes with the names of the patriarchs (Abraham, Isaac, etc.), prophets (major and minor, e.g. Elijah, Zephaniah, etc.) and saints (e.g. Columba, Aidan, Mary, etc.) on them. Make sure that you have more than you need, in order to cover the whole of the cardboard church.

Now give each person a brick shape and ask them to write their name on it. Also give out the brick shapes with the names of patriarchs, prophets and saints on them.

The congregation are going to stick their bricks on the cardboard church – but the question is, where will they stick the bricks? Should the patriarchs and saints go near the bottom? Should new Christians be near the top? Encourage the congregation to decide. Then, making sure that you have plenty of glue, ask everyone to come and place their bricks where they think they should go. Try not to knock the whole edifice down, and help those who are smaller in height to reach the top of the church, as necessary.

☐ *Music*

Sing 'For I'm making a people of power' (*Mission Praise*), or 'The church's one foundation' (*Mission Praise*).

THE SIXTH SUNDAY OF EASTER

Jesus gave his disciples a new commandment, and he gives the same to us: Love God, and love your neighbour as yourself.

Genesis 8.20—9.17
1 Peter 3.13–22 or Acts 17.22–31
John 14.15–21

- Old Testament survey for all the congregation.
- Pencils or pens.
- OHP or flip chart and fat pen.

☐ *Starter*

Before the service create an 'Old Testament Commandments Survey', for every member of the congregation, as in the illustration.

○ ○ ○ ○ ○ ○ ○ ○ ○ ○ ○ ○

OLD TESTAMENT COMMANDMENT'S
SURVEY

Put a √ against any commandments that you
have no trouble obeying
Put a **X** against any commandments that you
have trouble obeying
Put a **?** against any commandments that you
are not sure about

Be as honest as possible. No one else will see your survey.

- I am the Lord your God...
  you shall have no other gods before me
- You shall not make for yourself an idol
- You shall not make wrongful use of the
  name of the Lord your God
- Observe the Sabbath day and keep it holy
- Honour your father and mother
- Neither shall you commit adultery
- Neither shall you steal
- Neither shall you bear false witness
  against your neighbour
- Neither shall you covet (desire)

Give everyone in the congregation a copy of the Old Testament Commandments Survey and a pen or pencil. Inform them that the survey will remain anonymous, and they should be as honest as possible. Encourage adults and children to work together where appropriate.

Allow a few moments for everyone to complete the survey and then discuss the survey generally. You might want to ask the following questions:

- Did the survey cause any problems?
- Were there some commandments that it was simple to say you have no trouble in obeying? (Which were these? e.g. Do not commit murder)
- Were there some commandments that it was harder to say yes to? (Which were these? e.g. Do not covet, or Observe the Sabbath)
- What about the commandment that says, 'You should not make for yourself an idol'? What things might be considered idols in today's world?

☐ *Comment*

In the Gospel reading Jesus says, 'If you love me, you will keep my commandments' (John 14.15); and again, 'They who have my commandments and keep them are those who love me; and those who love me will be loved by my Father, and I will love them and reveal myself to them' (John 14.21). We have looked at the Ten Commandments that God gave to Moses and his people after their exodus from Egypt. Does Jesus mean these are the commandments that we are to obey?

Jesus gave us two specific commands, as well as a number of other instructions, during his three years of ministry with his disciples. The most important of these is what is often called the Great Commandment. A scribe asked Jesus the question, 'Which commandment is the first of all?' and Jesus replied:

> The first is, 'Hear, O Israel: the Lord our God, the Lord is one; you shall love the Lord your God with all your heart, and with all your soul, and with all your mind, and with all your strength.' The second is this, 'You shall love your neighbour as yourself.' There is no other commandment greater than these. (Mark 12.29–31)

For Jesus the greatest of all commands must be to love God, but equally if we love our fellow human beings as we love ourselves then we shall not need any other commandments, for all of the other nine commandments will be covered.

☐   *Conclusion*

Jesus gave us a number of other instructions. Look now at some of these. Put some of them up onto an OHP or flip chart and explore with the congregation what they might mean in a modern context.

JESUS' INSTRUCTIONS

'Go therefore and make disciples of all nations' (Matthew 28.19).
'Whoever blasphemes against the Holy Spirit can never have forgiveness' (Mark 3.29).
'There is nothing outside a person that by going in can defile, but the things that come out are what defile' (Mark 7.15).
'If any want to become my followers, let them deny themselves and take up their cross and follow me' (Mark 8.34b).
'All things can be done for the one who believes' (Mark 9.23b)
'Whoever welcomes one such child in my name welcomes me, and whoever welcomes me welcomes not me but the one who sent me' (Mark 9.37).
'If any of you put a stumbling block before one of these little ones who believe in me, it would be better for you if a great millstone were hung around your neck and you were thrown into the sea' (Mark 9.42).
'Love your enemies, do good to those who hate you, bless those who curse you, pray for those who abuse you' (Luke 6.27–28).
'Do not judge, and you will not be judged' (Luke 6.37).
'Do not worry about your life, what you will eat, or about your body, what you will wear' (Luke 12.22).

You might want to ask the following questions:

- Are there any commands or instructions here that you do not understand?
- Are there any that you find easy/difficult/impossible?
- Is there any way that we as a congregation could help one another to keep any or some of these instructions?
- Do you feel that you could take one or two away with you to work on over the next few weeks/months?

Have a time of silent prayer to allow individuals to offer their commitments to God.

ASCENSION DAY

Some myths about the ascension of Jesus are explored to try to understand this mysterious happening.

Daniel 7.9–14
Ephesians 1.15–23 or Acts 1.1–11
Luke 24.44–53

- Large sheets of paper and fat pens for each group.
- Scrap paper.
- Copy of the sayings using 'Up', with one on each sheet.
- OHP or flip chart.
- List of phrases with cartoon pictures.

☐ *Starter*

Before the service copy as many of the following phrases as you wish onto individual sheets of paper. Divide the congregation into small groups of up to six people. Children can work together with the help of an adult if they wish. Give each group a large sheet of paper and a fat pen. They might also need some scrap paper.

SAYINGS USING THE WORD 'UP'
Uptight
Back-up
Fed up
Moving up
Upset
Stir up
Fry up
Put up with
Shut up
Belt up
Put someone up to something
Buck up your ideas
Look something up
Growing up
Set up
Up the Rovers
Screw up

Explain that for many people the ascension is all about Jesus *going up* to heaven, which has caused many difficulties over our understanding of heaven. (For example, children sometimes ask, 'Is heaven beyond the solar system?') So today, we shall look at other meanings for the word 'up'.

Read the account of the ascension as told in St Luke's Gospel (Luke 24.50–51), before dividing the congregation into small groups of four to six people. Give each group a large sheet of paper, a fat pen, and one phrase from the sayings using the word 'up'. Their task is to draw a picture to describe their phrase. Do not write the word or phrase on the picture. If groups want to try out some draft versions first give them some small pieces of paper and pencils.

Now ask the congregation to notice that the word 'up' in the phrases at which they have looked rarely means 'upwards'. It sometimes means 'changed', however. Comment that we have many phrases which imply 'up', and these are associated with, or mean, something that is better. Put up on an OHP or flip chart some phrases and pictures prepared beforehand.

☐ *Comment*

As we have seen the word 'up' often means some kind of change, or something that is better. Is that not why we place Olympic winners on podiums, with the winner on the highest step? The opposite, down, is often seen as being a change for the worse. For example, phrases such as 'Take him down a peg' or 'That fish and chip shop is not as good as it was – it's gone downhill' both infer something negative.

So if we talk of someone going 'up to heaven' or 'up to God' we don't necessarily mean that they are physically being raised up into the sky. We often mean that they are being raised to a better position. Our ancestors did not know how to write about Jesus' ascension. It is after all a mystery. What they did know was that Jesus was being rewarded for his work. They believed that he would join his Father and be crowned as King of kings, and Lord of lords. Perhaps that is why Luke, writing at the end of his Gospel says:

> While he was blessing them, he withdrew from them (Luke 24.51)

The final words 'and was carried up into heaven' were, it seems, added much later.

☐ *Conclusion*

Look at all of the pictures without words attached, encourage the congregation to guess what the word or phrase might be. Finally, attach the correct word or phrase.

THE SEVENTH SUNDAY OF EASTER

We are witnesses today of the power of God in our lives, and as witnesses we need to speak out to others.

Ezekiel 36.24–28
1 Peter 4.12–14; 5.6–11 or Acts 1.6–14
John 17.1–11

- Characters to carry out the role play: witness and two police officers.
- A desk.
- Three chairs.
- Witness slips for all the congregation.
- Pens or pencils.

☐ *Starter*

Set up a role play of two police officers interviewing a slightly reluctant witness. The policemen or -women should sit behind a table, with the witness on the other side. Use the following, as appropriate.

INCIDENT

- The witness has seen two youths robbing the local newsagents. He was outside the shop, just about to go in as they were leaving.
- The owner of the shop, Mr Jones, was badly beaten and is in hospital.
- The youths confronted the witness and threatened him to keep his mouth shut, or they would deal with him.

Questions by police officers

- Confirm witness's name and address.
- Confirm the date and time of the incident.
- Confirm what he actually saw:
  – Did he actually see the youths robbing the till?
  – Did he actually see Mr Jones being beaten?
- Get witness to describe the two men.
  – Give a description of each youth (the detectives should tease each part of the description out of the witness – What colour was his hair? How tall exactly was he? etc.
  – What were the youths wearing?
  – Describe their voices and mannerisms
- Were there any other people around to witness the incident?

The witness should be slightly reluctant (although does give the information required) perhaps because he is not quite sure what he has seen, or because he feels he might be in danger. End with a police officer thanking the witness, perhaps with a comment such as: 'It's a pity more witnesses aren't as forthcoming as you have been, sir.'

□ Comment

As we have seen being a witness is not a simple thing. None of us is good at recalling exactly every detail of something that has happened. How tall is someone? What were the features of their face? Sometimes we would have trouble in describing a loved one, never mind someone we have only seen for a moment or two and in the middle of a terrifying incident.

Then there is the courage needed to be a witness. Mr? knows that he might well be in danger from the two youths. They may know who he is, or be able to find out his address in some way. What if they attack his family? If he stands up as a witness he lays himself open to all of this. Besides this, it also requires courage to make a statement and to stand up in court in the full glare of the media to accuse someone else. What if he is wrong? Perhaps he was mistaken?

In the reading from the Acts of the Apostles today we see Jesus taking his farewell from his disciples. His final instruction is this:

> '. . . you will receive power when the Holy Spirit has come upon you; and you will be my witnesses in Jerusalem, in all Judea and Samaria, and to the ends of the earth.' (Acts 1.8)

They are to be witnesses to all that they have seen and heard in the three years they have been with Jesus. They will need to recall every detail of what has happened; they will need to have courage to speak to individuals and to courts and kings; they will need to put thoughts of themselves and their own danger on one side in order to witness effectively.

St Matthew's Gospel makes it even plainer. Here Jesus is quoted as saying:

> 'Go therefore and make disciples of all nations, baptizing them in the name of the Father and of the Son and of the Holy Spirit.' (Matthew 28.19)

The apostles' task was clear – they were to witness to Jesus' life and work, and make disciples. These disciples would then continue God's work. We are the natural inheritors of this work, for we too have received the Holy Spirit and are Christ's disciples. We are called to witness to Jesus Christ, to bravely go and tell others of what we have learnt and experienced. We are today's witnesses!

□ Conclusion

Give each person in the congregation a Witness Statement, and a pen or pencil. Encourage young children to work with adults. Ask the congregation to list the ways that God is at work in their lives, e.g. I have faith; I feel peace when I turn to God; he helps me to overcome my faults, etc.

```
••• WITNESS STATEMENT •••

I .................................................................. (name)


    ..............................................................


    ..............................................................


    ..............................................................


    ..............................................................


    ..............................................................
```

The Witness Statements may be gathered in and offered at the altar, although it might be better if everyone was allowed to take the statements home and continue working on them.

PENTECOST

The Holy Spirit gives his gifts to individuals, according to their needs. These gifts are always for the benefit of the community.

Numbers 11.24–30
1 Corinthians 12.3b–13 or Acts 2.1–21
John 20.19–23 or John 7.37–39

- Three or four unsuitable presents and people primed to receive them.
- Spiritual Gifts sheet for everyone.
- Pens or pencils.
- *Optional:* Collage of those who work for the church, or a list of jobs in the church.

□ *Starter*

Choose four or five very unsuitable presents for four or five members of the congregation, for example:

- A pair of hiking boots for a couch potato.
- A book by Stephen Hawking for a small child.

Wrap the gifts up as presents. However, forewarn the people you have chosen, so that they can show suitable thankfulness, but bewilderment, when they are given the presents.

Explore with your helpers what is wrong with the presents. Why don't they like them? What would they have preferred?

□ *Comment*

I did not choose my presents very well. I didn't really think about the people concerned and what they might have wanted. The secret of a good 'giver' is someone who spends time thinking about the person. What are their hobbies? What would they like? Unfortunately, all too often we think about what we would like, and give our friends the present *we* would like to have received.

The secret of God's gift to us is that it is a gift just for us. It is a gift tailored for us. When the disciples received the Holy Spirit at Pentecost it was to receive a gift that was fitted to each one of them. The Holy Spirit enabled them to do all kinds of things. Some were to become preachers, some teachers, and some prophets. Not all would become preachers, not all would become teachers, and not all would become prophets. St Paul was to list some of these gifts: the utterance of wisdom, the utterance of knowledge, faith, healing, and the working of miracles. Each person would be given the gift suited to them.

However, what we should notice is that the Holy Spirit gives his gifts to Christians for the benefit of the *community*. They are never given to benefit a person. It is not like winning the lottery. The gift is always to be used to help the church community or the wider community in the world. As Christians we are not primarily individuals, we are a community, which is why we cannot be a Christian apart from the church community.

☐ *Conclusion*

Before the service produce a list of the spiritual gifts that St Paul refers to, as follows.

SPIRITUAL GIFTS

St Paul says that the Holy Spirit gives us spiritual gifts:

- ability to speak wisdom
- knowledge to help others
- faith
- ability to heal others
- ability to work miracles
- ability to prophesy
- ability to discern good and evil
- ability to speak in tongues
- ability to interpret tongues
- ability to teach others
- ability to assist others
- ability to lead others

Which of these do you think you possess?
How do you use your gift to help others?
Do you think God has given you other gifts? If so, what?

....

Give out the Spiritual Gifts sheet. Allow people some time to think about the gifts. Then close with the prayer.

☐ *Optional*

Create a collage on all the people who work for your church: the churchwardens or deacons, the sacristan, the choir leader, etc.

Or, invite people to stand up in their place as you call out all the jobs, this will allow them to choose which they stand for, since some people will carry out many tasks. Make sure you leave nothing out, or someone will be upset, but equally refer to those who cannot do much work because of job or health circumstances. End with 'Those who pray for others'. This should ensure almost everyone (including those who are too busy at home or work, or who are unwell) stands up. If there are visitors you might want to ask them about their own church, if this is appropriate, or simply just welcome them. It might also be a good opportunity to see who could take on some more work.

TRINITY SUNDAY

The Trinity is three, yet one, and we need to hold the balance as equal between the different aspects of God.

Genesis 1.1—2.4a or Isaiah 40.12–17, 27–31
2 Corinthians 13.11–13
Matthew 28.16–20

- Group leaders.
- Bible references.
- Craft materials.

☐ *Starter*

In the week before the service appoint three leaders to be responsible for creating some work on:

- God the Creator
- God the Son
- God the Holy Spirit

Each leader is to gather more helpers according to the size of the congregation. They will be working with groups of about six people. Their task is to look at the aspect of God they have been given, and to explore the following:

- To create a simple explanation of God the Father/Mother (or God the Son, etc.).
- To find evidence of his work or life in the Old and New Testament (for Jesus, look at the prophecies *and* the Gospels).
- To produce some creative work to show his work or influence.
- To do some serious thinking about how the Trinity would be diminished without this Person.

The leaders are to gather as much material as possible (books, posters, craft materials) and be as imaginative as possible, but they are not to do the work for the congregation. One exception might be to create a list of Bible references, so that individuals can start by looking them up.

BIBLE REFERENCES

God

Numbers 14.18a	Psalm 36.7
Psalm 46.1	Psalm 100.5
Psalm 103.13–14	Psalm 147.6
Isaiah 40.8	John 3.16–17
John 4.24	Romans 5.8
Romans 8.31b–32	Hebrews 4.12
1 John 4.16b	Revelations 1.8

Jesus

Isaiah 7.14	Isaiah 9.6
Isaiah 11.1–2	Isaiah 11.10
Micah 5.2	Luke 2.10–11
Luke 2.19–20	Matthew 3.13, 16–17
Matthew 7.28–29	Mark 7.37
Luke 9.1–2	John 6.35
John 8.12	John 12.12–13
John 19.15b–16	1 Corinthians 11.23b–25
Romans 8.34b	

Holy Spirit

Genesis 1.1–2	Numbers 11.24–25
Numbers 27.18–19	Judges 13.24–25a
Matthew 1.18	Matthew 3.16
Matthew 4.1	John 14.15–17
John 14.26	John 16.13
Romans 5.5b	Galatians 5.22–23a
1 Corinthians 12.4–5	1 John 4.13

□ *Conclusion*

When everyone has finished allow time for everyone to look at the work, then hear back from as many groups as possible. Encourage them to 'fight for their corner', and to show the importance of their aspect of God to the Trinity.

□ *Comment*

On Trinity Sunday we remember the three-ness of God: God as Father or Creator, God as the Son, and God as the Holy Spirit. God is one, but he is also three. Each aspect of God, as we have seen, is a vital part of the very being of God.

God the Father created the world. The plan for redeeming humanity was his. He it was to whom Jesus prayed. God the Son is Jesus who lived as a man, and who finally gave his life to bring us back into a living relationship with his Father. God the Holy Spirit is the power source of God in our world. Without him the church would not exist.

Sometimes, however, we put too great an emphasis on one aspect of the Trinity. For instance, we concentrate too much on Jesus, forgetting that he always emphasized his Father. Nothing was done except through God the Father. Or we find we can identify with God as Father, but have difficulty with Jesus. We need to try and keep the three aspects of the Trinity in balance, as God does himself.

PROPER 4

Sunday between 29 May and 4 June (if after Trinity Sunday)

Jesus says we must do the will of God, his Father. This week explores what it means to 'do God's will'.

Genesis 6.9–22; 7.24; 8.14–19
Romans 1.16–17; 3.22b–28 (29–31)
Matthew 7.21–29

- Clues and artefacts for the two hunts – see lists below.

☐ *Starter*

Jesus says that not everyone will enter the kingdom of heaven, only those 'who do the will of my Father'. Organize two hunts with texts and artefacts for adults and children.

You will need to hide the following items inside and, where possible, outside the church. Alongside these put the texts as shown. To ensure the adults and children can find their clues write the texts on different coloured papers. Note that the children's texts are traditional phrases about Jesus, to encourage them to become familiar with them. Parents or other adults can explain some of them to the children as appropriate.

ARTEFACTS AND TEXTS FOR ADULTS

- Pair of scales: Matthew 7.1.
- A white cloth: Matthew 5.8.
- A picture of two adults: Matthew 5.22a.
- A picture of a mother and a child: Matthew 10.37.
- A picture of an altar (or the text simply on the altar): Matthew 5.23–24.
- A log of wood: Matthew 7.3–5.
- A picture of a famine victim or someone in prison: Matthew 25.41, 44–45.
- A text pinned onto a Bible or the lectern: Matthew 7.24–25.
- Two wedding rings placed on a copy of the wedding service: Matthew 5.28.
- A crucifix or cross: Matthew 12.31.
- Some rotting food (or a picture of rotting food): Matthew 15.11.
- A picture of someone with a knife or gun, or a picture of war: Matthew 5.44.
- A picture of a baby or small child: Matthew 18.3–4.

Artefacts and texts for children

- A traditional picture of Jesus: John 3.36.
- A loaf of bread: John 6.35.
- A glass of water: John 7.37b.
- A big lighted candle, or a lamp: John 9.5b.
- A picture of a sheep, or a toy sheep: John 10.11a.
- A picture of children, happy together: John 15.12.

Give the adults Bibles or New Testaments. The children could use children's Bibles, as desired. Inform both adults and children what colour paper their texts are written on, and send them off to find all the texts. Make sure they understand that they should leave both the artefacts and the texts where they find them, so that everyone has a chance of looking up the instructions.

☐ *Optional*
Read the story of the two houses (Matthew 7.24–27) to younger children. Explain its meaning, and then create a collage based on the story.

☐ *Comment*
Jesus taught some hard lessons to his disciples, and in turn he teaches them to us. For those of us who think it is sufficient to call

Jesus 'Lord', or who think it sufficient to attend church each week, then Jesus has a harsh awakening.

> Not everyone who says to me, 'Lord, Lord,' will enter the kingdom of heaven, but only one who does the will of my Father in heaven. (Matthew 7.21)

As we have seen to 'do God's will' requires us to do more than worship God, or even to say the right words. We have to live a lifestyle that reflects our beliefs. If we come to the altar but have not forgiven another person for some slight, then we are at fault. If we join the Bible study group, but spend the whole time being critical of another person, then we are at fault. The way we think and the way we behave as Christians needs overhauling.

When we do God's will, Jesus says, we are like a man who built his house on a rock. When the storm comes the house stands firm.

☐ *Conclusion*

Hear back from both groups about their experiences. Did they find all the texts and articles? Did they have difficulties?

☐ *Music*

Sing 'The wise man built his house upon the rock' (*Junior Praise*).

PROPER 5

Sunday between 5 June and 11 June (if after Trinity Sunday)

Jesus calls all people to follow him. No one in our community is beyond his loving care.

Genesis 12.1–9
Romans 4.13–25
Matthew 9.9–13, 18–26

- Group leaders.
- OHP or flip chart and fat pen.
- Paper and pencils.
- Large sheet of paper and a fat pen for each group.

□ *Comment*

In St Matthew's Gospel we see Jesus calling a most unlikely
candidate to be his disciple. This calling also appears to come much
later than the call to the fishermen from Galilee. Matthew is a tax
collector and one of the most hated of men. It is somewhat difficult
now to imagine quite how hated they were, but we need to
remember that they worked for the enemy, the Romans, who had
conquered the Jewish nation. Not only this but many tax collectors
demanded more than they actually paid to the Romans, so making
themselves enormous profits.

Presumably Jesus had met Matthew before, but the call must still
have come as a surprise. The greater surprise though was that Jesus
would sit at a meal and eat with men like Matthew – men who
were outcasts and unclean. No self-respecting Jew would normally
do such a thing, for it would make him ritually unclean. But Jesus
wants to associate with those who are beyond the pale of normal
society. It is to such people as these that he has come with a
message of love. The poor, the wretched, the prisoner, and the
unloved are all wanted by Jesus, the Son of God.

□ *Starter*

In the week before the service appoint group leaders. Each leader
will have up to eight people in their group.

Using an OHP or flip chart invite the congregation to think of
how many different groups there are in your parish or area. For
example:

- The elderly
- Children
- The under-fives
- Prisoners
- Men
- Shoppers, etc.

Make as comprehensive a list as possible.

□ *Conclusion*

Now create groups of up to eight people. Children may choose to
stay with adults, or have a group(s) of their own. Each group will
need a large sheet of paper and a fat pen. The task of the leaders is
to help their group look at how the church might take the gospel to
different people in their area. Each group should be given one of
the categories already identified. More than one group can look at
the same category.

Groups should come up with as many practical ways as possible
of contacting and working with the category of people with which
they are concerned. For example:

- Deliver leaflets inviting people to church.
- Visit to invite people to church.
- Put on some special event.
- Offer some particular service (e.g. a sale of children's clothes, or a social evening).

Put group decisions onto the large sheet of paper. Finally, appoint one person to keep hold of the information and act as a co-ordinator. Put up the group's conclusions for all to view. After the service arrange to meet with the other co-ordinators and to continue working on the material. Look at all the suggestions again and make plans for the future. Take the plans to the Church Council, and finally start working on one of the easy and one of the more difficult suggestions.

PROPER 6

Sunday between 12 June and 18 June (if after Trinity Sunday)

Jesus says, 'The harvest is plentiful, but the labourers are few.' A study of the disciples helps us to look once more at vocations to the ministry.

Genesis 18.1–15 (21.1–7)
Romans 5.1–8
Matthew 9.35—10.8 (9–23)

- Texts for looking at the individual disciples.
- Large sheets of paper and fat pens, or OHP or flip chart.

☐ *Starter*

Divide the congregation into groups, and allocate the name of a disciple to each group. Give out the Bible texts (see below). Where there are a number of references for one of the disciples create large groups and divide the texts up within the group. Give each group some paper, and pens or pencils.

The task for each group is to find out as much as they can about each disciple. Jesus chose these men to send the good news to all the world. The groups will need to look at:

- Their background.
- What strengths they had.
- What gifts they brought to the job.
- What made them special.

  □ *Optional*

Read some stories about the disciples to younger children from a
children's Bible.

DISCIPLES

Peter

Matthew 10.2–5	Matthew 14.29
Matthew 26.69–75	Mark 1.29–31
Mark 8.29	Luke 5.1–11
Luke 9.1–6	Luke 9.28–36
Luke 22.7–13	John 13.3–11
John 13.21–25	John 20.1–10
Acts 1.15–26	Acts 2.14–36
Acts 3.1–end	Acts 4.1–5
Acts 4.6–22	Acts 8.14–25
Acts 10.1–end	Acts 12.1–end
Acts 15.7–11	Galatians 2.14

Andrew

Matthew 4.18–20	Mark 1.29
Mark 13.3–4	Luke 9.1–6
John 1.35–42	John 6.5–9
John 12.20–23	Acts 1.12–13

James

Matthew 10.2	Matthew 17.1–8
Mark 1.19–20	Mark 14.32–42
Luke 5.10–11	Luke 9.1–6
Acts 12.1–3	

John

Matthew 20.20–23	Mark 1.19–20
Luke 5.10–11	Luke 9.1–6
Luke 9.49–50	Luke 22.7–13
John 19.26–27	John 13.23–26
John 20.1–10	Acts 1.12–14
Acts 3—4	Acts 8.14–17

Philip

Matthew 10.1–6	Luke 9.1–6
John 1.43–46	John 12.20–23

John 14.8–11   Acts 1.13–14
Acts 8.4–13   Acts 8.26–40

Bartholomew

Matthew 10.2–6   Luke 9.1–6
Acts 1.12–14

Matthew

Matthew 9.9   Mark 3.14–19
Luke 9.1–6   Acts 1.12–14

Thomas

Matthew 10.2–4   Luke 9.1–6
John 11.11–16   John 14.1–7
John 20.24–29   John 21.1–14
Acts 1.12–14

James, the son of Alphaeus

Matthew 10.2–4   Luke 9.1–6
Acts 1.12–14

Simon, the Zealot
Matthew 10.2–4   Luke 6.13–16
Luke 9.1–6

Judas (also known as Jude, Thaddeus, and Lebbaeus)

Luke 6.13–16   Luke 9.1–6
John 14.22–24   Acts 1.12–14

 ☐ *Conclusion*
When the groups have read through the Bible references for each
disciple they should begin to gather the information together. What
does it say about their disciple? What are his strengths and
weaknesses? What kind of a character was he? This could be
brainstormed onto a sheet of paper.

Bring the whole congregation back together and go through each
disciple. Either invite groups to speak from their sheets of paper, or
using an OHP or flip chart gather the main characteristics of each
man.

From the evidence make conclusions about what a person needs
to become a disciple of Jesus. Keep these as simple and realistic as
possible.

 ☐ *Comment*
In the ninth and tenth chapters of St Matthew's Gospel we see Jesus
surrounded by people, all of whom want something from him.

Many of them are sick, and sickness was considered by the Jewish people to be symptomatic of sinfulness. Whether this accelerated Jesus' plans we have no way of knowing. But it is at this time that we see him sending out the 12 disciples.

The disciples are ordinary working men: fishermen, a tax collector, and a Jewish zealot. They are not trained evangelists, they are not slick communicators, or even experienced rabbis. They are simply very ordinary men. Jesus takes the most raw material and begins to shape it into something he can use. We only have to compare the disciples before and after the resurrection to see the difference that will occur.

If a managing director today had taken such raw material for such a huge project we would think him or her mad. But it is the nature of Christianity that Christ takes our rawness and moulds us into his people. Our task today is to take note of the characteristics that we found important for discipleship (e.g. faith, willingness to leave the old life behind, etc.) and to discern those within our congregation who have a calling to discipleship. Who are those who are called to be priests/readers/deacons in our congregation? The process of discerning vocations is always led by the Holy Spirit, but it takes men and women to say, 'Don't you think God is calling you to be a . . . ?'

Remember Jesus' words apply just as much today as 2,000 years ago:

> 'The harvest is plentiful, but the labourers are few; therefore ask the Lord of the harvest to send out labourers into his harvest.' (Matthew 9.37–38)

 ☐ *Prayers*

Include prayers for those in training for the ministry, for evangelists and missioners, for forthcoming ordinations, and for the discernment of vocations within the church.

PROPER 7

Sunday between 19 June and 25 June (if after Trinity Sunday)

Christians need to look at their non-Christian neighbours in a different way, and also show that Christianity has something to offer them.

Genesis 21.8–21
Romans 6.1b–11
Matthew 10.24–39

- OHP, transparencies of pictures, or a number of copies of pictures of A3 size.
- Copies of the two stories.

☐   *Starter*

Gather together a number of pictures that can be seen in two ways. You will need an OHP, or many copies of the pictures (see Appendix). The most common of these pictures is the Necker cube, the old woman or the young woman, and the duck or the rabbit, but there are many others.

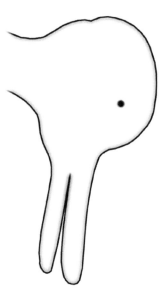

A reversal figure created by the cartoonist W. E. Hill in 1915.
The young woman's chin is the old woman's nose.

Invite the congregation to look at the pictures. What do they see first? Can they be encouraged to see both pictures. With the Necker cube there are three ways of seeing it: as a box with a corner facing you, as a box with a side facing you in diamond form, and as a flat non-three-dimensional 'badge'. Invite those who can see the alternate pictures to explain to the congregation what they are seeing.

It will take some considerable time for the congregation to get most of the pictures. You might also want to tell stories to help people see the other pictures, as below.

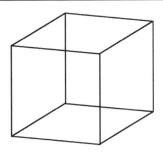

Necker cube

As a society we have been brought up to see cubes everywhere and they are nothing unusual to us. But imagine that you had never seen a cube. Don Ihde, an American working on the way we see things tells the story of a tribe of Indians living in the Amazon rainforest who have never seen a cube. However, they do have a symbol that is important to them. It is an insect with six legs. The tribe have made badges to represent this insect. The badges are hexagonal shapes, with the body of the insect in the middle and the six legs touching the sides of the hexagon.

Picture of Jesus

Once upon a time there was a man who feared flying. He would do anything to avoid flying. But the day came when he could no longer avoid it, and he was forced to travel abroad for his work.

He dreaded the plane taking off, he dreaded the plane flying above the clouds, and worst of all he dreaded the plane coming down. He also knew that he would spend the whole of the week worrying about the flight home rather than concentrating on his work.

Well, he survived the plane taking off, mostly by just closing his eyes and concentrating on something else. But just as he was beginning to relax a little and dinner was served, he accidentally glanced out of the window. Below him were the gigantic peaks of the Swiss mountains. His stomach heaved. He almost stopped breathing in his panic. He closed his eyes, then despite himself opened them again to look out of the window. Had it been his imagination? Or had he really seen something truly amazing? No, it was true. He had seen the face of Christ on the ground below.

Never again would he worry about flying. He would put his trust in God.

□　*Comment*

Jesus calls us to take his word to all people. For he warns that 'whoever denies me before others, I also will deny before my Father in heaven' (Matthew 10.33). The burden is on us to continue to speak out to the world, for the world's sake.

However, our society is very secular. It sees things in only one light, and unless concrete proof is given nothing is believed. We demand instant gratification and cannot wait; we cannot save money for what we want, but would prefer it instantly. Consequently we rely heavily on credit rather than on savings. Young couples who marry must have everything perfect in their dream house from the beginning, rather than work and plan to achieve it eventually.

Second, our society teaches us that the only thing which matters is personal gratification. I am the person that matters, others do not. What I want is of prime importance, and 'give me' is the cry of the day.

All of this is the complete opposite to what Christianity teaches, and leaves Christians feeling like outsiders. Consequently we can become somewhat dogmatic in what we teach. 'This is the way', we argue. 'You must do this.' God calls us to go out into the world and take his message to the people. To do that we need to understand the people to whom we go. Jesus didn't preach to the outcast, he went and had a meal with them. So we need to look at others in new ways, and we need to encourage them to see Christianity in a new light. It is all too easy to think you know about Christianity

from the outside (when in fact you know little) and it is all too easy
to make wrong assumptions about people who are not Christians.

☐ *Conclusion*

Divide the congregation into twos. Invite them to tell each other
something of their life, for example:

- a time of great joy
- a time of great sorrow
- a time of great difficulty

Allow two or three minutes for *each* person to speak. Encourage
them to tell the story in as much detail as possible. While the
account is being told the listener should not speak at all. However
when the speaker has finished the listener should now tell the
speaker how they are feeling. Concentrate on *feelings*, not on the
action of the story. Try to get inside the other person and
understand how they feel. For example:

A TIME OF GREAT JOY

Madge The day of my daughter's wedding was a wonderful
day. The sun shone, all the family arrived in time. I
cried when I saw my daughter dressed, she looked so
beautiful. I remembered when she had been a small
girl and liked dressing up as a bride, and now here
she was about to get married.

When Mary walked down the aisle and stood by
Tom, I was so proud of them both. They looked
wonderful . . .

Jennie [*responding afterwards*] So you felt that the whole day
was very special, and that Mary looked wonderful.
You remembered how she had pretended to be a
bride when she was a young girl. You felt very proud
of her and of Tom when you saw them in church.

PROPER 8

Sunday between 26 June and 2 July

What kind of a welcome do we give newcomers and tourists? Do we make children really welcome? These are some of the questions explored this week.

Genesis 22.1–14
Romans 6.12–23
Matthew 10.40–42

> - 2 speakers (electoral roll officer/new Christian).
> - OHP or flip chart and fat pen.
> - A group of children.
> - *Optional:* Children's leader.

☐ *Starter*

As a whole congregation, look at your church from an outsider's point of view. Try not to antagonize anyone, but be as realistic as possible. You might want to look at some of the following:

- Invite the electoral roll officer/church membership secretary to speak about the trends in your church. How many people have left (including death!) or joined in the last two or three years. If possible produce a graph on an OHP or flip chart showing the age ranges of those who are church members. What conclusions can be drawn from this?
- How do you welcome newcomers? Do you have a 'welcomer' available at each service? Do you invite people to fill out a slip giving their name and address? Are these names passed on to a minister or visitor and followed up? Do you have parish or church magazines to pass on to newcomers? If you never get any newcomers, what would you do if one appeared?
- Do you ever receive visitors (as opposed to newcomers) because of the area in which you live? How do you welcome tourists? Are there leaflets about the church available? Have you appointed someone to be responsible for work with tourists?
- Do you greet new families or children? Do you have a box or bag of quiet toys available for young children? Is there anyone available to help parents by sitting with young children or playing with them? Are there suitable books for children to read?

Is there a corner that they can be taken to if things get difficult?
Is there some part of the service specifically suitable for children,
and if not why not?

- Do you (the congregation) actually speak to newcomers or
tourists?
- How do you help newcomers who may not be accustomed to
church to know when to stand up, sit down, or find their place in
the prayer book?
- Ask someone, or a family, to speak about their experience of first
coming to your church.

You may want to add other questions to those above.

□ *Comment*

Jesus says that 'whoever welcomes you welcome me, and whoever
welcomes me welcomes the one who sent me' (Matthew 10.40). In
welcoming people to church (and to our homes!) we are actually
welcoming God into our church (and home).

Sometimes we have been a part of a church for so long that we
do not see it from the outside. We forget how difficult it is to
actually step over the threshold, and how frightening it is to find
ourselves in an unfamiliar situation with people who all know each
other and who know how to behave. Perhaps we need to think of
what it might be like for us to visit a temple or shrine belonging to
another faith on our own. It is surely no different for the newcomer.
A welcoming smile or handshake and an unintrusive enquiry can
make all the difference as to whether we return.

Some of our habits in church are not conducive to welcoming
newcomers or tourists. We tend to want children to sit down and be
quiet, so that we can concentrate on our own worship, and while
this might be acceptable on one level, it is very hurtful to the
parents of young children. So we need to think of ways that we can
help parents feel welcome while still encouraging a suitable
atmosphere for worship. A give-and-take relationship needs to be
developed between those with and those without children. Not all
parents may want to put their children in a crèche, and in this case
they will need help rather than censure.

If we give people a true welcome when they come to church, we
shall pass on the love that God gives to us.

□ *Conclusion*

Invite the children in your church to tell the adults what they
like, and what they don't like about church. This might be done
by creating small groups, to include the children. They may be so
indoctrinated about 'going out of the service' that they see
nothing wrong with it, but adults need to remember how they

would feel if they were 'sent out to learn' rather than 'kept in to worship'.

Alternatively ask those who work with children to talk about their experience of working with the children. Are there ways that the congregation could help to link the children's work and the adults' work together so that the children seamlessly move from Junior Church or Sunday School to the normal morning or evening worship?

PROPER 9

Sunday between 3 July and 9 July

All of us experience times when we are down, and when life seems impossible. We need to learn to offload all our difficulties, and simply rest in God's arms.

Genesis 24.34–38, 42–49, 58–67
Romans 7.15–25a
Matthew 11.16–19, 25–30

- A speaker.

 □ *Starter*
Invite someone to come and speak of a time of great worry when all the troubles of the world seemed to be upon their shoulders, and of how they were helped by someone else. This could be a situation where they got into trouble (financial, or out of their depth in water, or couldn't get down a mountain), or it could be that they were diagnosed with a life-threatening illness which has subsequently been cured. You might want to set up an interview situation to help the speaker. Questions such as the following might help:

- Can you tell us what happened to you (last year/when you were young, etc.)?
- Where were you at the time?/How old were you at the time?
- Where were you living?

- Were you worried?/How did you feel?
- Who was with you?
- Who helped you?

Keep the interview purely on the human level of who helped, even if the person is a Christian. Make sure that everyone understands how awful the situation was, and how worrying it was at the time. Finally ask them how they felt when the situation was resolved.

 ☐ *Comment*
[*Adapt the following as appropriate*]
We have seen the hard time that ..... (*name of person who has been speaking*) had (this year/last year/when she was small), and of how she felt when it was resolved. I am sure we are all pleased that she is all right now, and we hope it will never happen again. She has given us, though, some idea of what it feels like to be rescued/cured when you have given up hope and thought that the end was there.

All of us have felt like this at some time in our lives. We have been frightened and out of our depth; we have felt that it was impossible to go on; or we have felt as if we were the only ones suffering in this way. It may last for just a few moments, or it may last for months. We have heard how ...... (*name of speaker*) felt when she was rescued/cured by ...... (*person who helped*). We have heard of her relief, and of how she felt free again. Sometimes people say that even colours seem brighter, and birds sing sweeter when they come out of such a black hole of depression.

Jesus says when we feel desperate we should come to him, and he will ease our soul.

> Come to me, all you that are weary and are carrying heavy burdens, and I will give you rest. (Matthew 11.28)

It doesn't mean that we shall always be rescued, but when we rest on him he will give us the strength to carry on. We are never alone even at the lowest points in our life. He is always there ready to step in and ease our burden.

 ☐ *Optional*
You could invite a speaker to give a testimony about how they have been able to offload all their difficulties onto God, even if they still have to live with the problem.

 ☐ *Conclusion*
Encourage everyone to turn to their neighbour(s) and talk about a time when they have been rescued, or when they have felt able to turn to God for solace.

☐ *Prayer*

Include prayer for all those facing difficult decisions, times of hardship, or particular dangers.

PROPER 10

Sunday between 10 July and 16 July

An exploration of the parable of the sower is carried out to look at how people come to faith, and at the roots of our own faith.

Genesis 25.19–34
Romans 8.1–11
Matthew 13.1–9, 18–23

> - Two leaders for the drama.
> - Copies of the drama suggestions.

☐ *Starter*

Create some drama or role play for the whole congregation. Children of all ages should join in. Encourage everyone to take part, but allow any who are unwilling, to be the audience.

Set up two difference pieces of drama, one the answer to the other. The first piece of drama is based on Matthew 13.3b–9, and the second on Matthew 13.18–23.

You will need two leaders (one for each piece of drama) capable of working with the congregation. You will also need two separate places to work. If no separate room is available try working with one group outside.

The following suggestions might be helpful.

- Read the parable and its explanation to the whole congregation. Now divide everyone into two groups. If your congregation is very large, then create four groups and produce two separate pieces of work.

Matthew 13.3b–9

- Carry out some work with this group on growing from a seed to a fully fledged ear of corn, e.g. start with them curled up in balls as the seed, then the sun comes up, and they grow just a tiny bit – perhaps the head lifts, etc. until they are standing with both arms waving. Also practise dying with all the seeds! Don't rush this part of the work, but encourage them to use their imagination. The elderly could be encouraged to remain seated while still acting.
- Appoint a sower, and two people to walk behind the sower, carrying the heavy bags of seed.
- Appoint some to act as birds.
- Appoint everyone else as seeds, and place them in four separate groups (as the seed on the path; the seed on the rocky ground; the seed in the thorns; and the seed in the good soil).
- If you have a very large group some could be appointed as thorns (in imaginary disjointed positions with the 'seed' below them).
- Finally try a dress rehearsal as follows, with all the seeds in curled up positions initially. The leader should read the words from Matthew 13.3b–9 at a suitable pace to allow the action to take place:
  – The farmer sows accompanied by two assistants carrying bags of seed.
  – The first group of seeds begin to grow, but the birds swoop in and start to devour them (and the seeds simply die).
  – The second group of seeds begin to grow very quickly but there is no water, and so after a quick burst of growth they die.
  – The third group of seeds are placed within the thorns, and as they grow the thorns simply smother them, and so they too die.
  – The fourth group of seeds begin to grow as the sower reaches them, and continue to grow into strong healthy plants.

Matthew 13.18–23

- Appoint one person as an evangelist. He or she is the speaker at a conference. All this is mime so they will need grand gestures, arm-waving and thumping the 'pulpit' to indicate their job. Appoint half of the group as listeners at the meeting. Appoint a few as people passing by, some of whom will get sucked into the meeting, some of whom will reject it and go on their way. Appoint the rest of the group as those who will draw the listeners away from the meeting.

- *Seed 1* Some of those listening at the meeting walk away, trying to understand the message – perhaps reading a Bible, but shaking their heads as they fail to understand. One or two might walk away with a friend who is trying to help them, however, they still fail to understand the message.
- *Seed 2* Next some of those listening react with over-the-top joy (arms waving, clapping, absolute ecstasy), and leave the group to try and explain this wonderful thing they have discovered to those who have already left. This group don't want to know and are pretty rough in rejecting them. Seed 2 give up and join the disaffected group.
- *Seed 3* Like Seed 2 they receive the message, but not so over-the-top. However, after a moment or two the disaffected group 2 entice them for a drink, to play cards, to return to work, or play football. Seed 3 have given up.
- *Seed 4* Like Seed 2 and 3 this group receives the message. They stay together as a group. One becomes ill and another helps them; one begins to explain to another what the Bible means; one is hungry and another takes them food, etc.

☐ *Conclusion*

Gather everyone together. Now read the two sections of the story again, this time accompanied by the drama. Encourage each group to watch and listen to each other's offering.

☐ *Comment*

The parable of the sower has a double message for us today. For the past few weeks we have been looking at evangelism and mission, at vocations, and at how we welcome people into church. This story reminds us of the way that people sometimes receive the message we take to them. Often they welcome our visit, but there is no basis for the word of God to take hold, and we never see or hear from them again. At other times they greet us like long-lost relatives and welcome the invitation to come to church. They join in everything that is going on and embrace everything with great excitement, but somehow it doesn't last. They get upset by something that is said or done, and before we know it they have left. The word of God never really got established in their hearts. Then there are those who join us but who get side-tracked by football on Sunday, or swimming classes, or even the family. Their faith never takes root in practice. Thank God, though, that some of those whom we visit embrace

Christianity wholeheartedly. Some through the baptism of a child, or because a loved one has died.

Whatever happens, if we have carried out our commission faithfully, and done God's work as best as we are able, we can stand proud. Sometimes, after all, the seed of God's word lies dormant, to be picked up later. If you speak to someone new in the faith they will often tell you that four or five events led to their becoming a Christian.

However there is a second way of looking at this parable. It can apply to us. We do not know how long some of the plants grew before they finally withered and died. We might be like that. We need to question our own faith, whether it is rooted and grounded deep in good soil. Is our faith based on Jesus himself, or is it based on something else, perhaps on the enjoyment of coming to church to meet our friends, or because we like the minister? Pray that our faith is grounded deeply in God.

PROPER 11

Sunday between 17 July and 23 July

How do we know if someone is bad? We shouldn't make judgements – only God judges. As a society we are quick to judge, and even quicker to demand punishment. But the gospel teaches us that good and evil are not always obvious. We need to remember not to judge, but to leave that to God.

Genesis 28.10–19a
Romans 8.12–25
Matthew 13.24–30, 36–43

- Large numbers of newspapers.
- Felt-tip pens.
- Possible need for an OHP or flip chart and pens.

☐ *Starter*
Gather as many newspapers together as possible. These can be of any date and any kind. The congregation can work together in

twos, or in small groups of any size. Give each group one or two newspapers.

Their task is to explore the newspaper for stories which are based on negative judgements taken by the paper or by society, for example:

- A story where society, or a newspaper, has decided that someone has made a mistake (e.g. a doctor, a footballer, etc.), even though there has been no court-case.
- A story where someone is deemed to be a wrong-doer without a trial (e.g. hooligans, a car driver, someone on a sex-offender list who has served their time, etc.).
- A story where the editor/the paper has decided to hound someone because of some action of theirs (a politician, etc.).

Mark each story with the letter A, and note for special attention later any judgements that you feel are unjustified. When this has been completed carry out the same task, but this time look at positive judgements taken by the paper or by society. Mark these with a letter B. Note any that seem unjustified.

Finally, add up the letters A and B. Which are the greater?

□ *Conclusion*

Gather all the judgements together and talk about them with the congregation. Is it possible to decide whether we are quicker to praise or blame? Comment on any that feel particularly unjustifiable. Do the congregation feel that there are any lessons to be learnt from this exercise about the way that we make judgements on others?

□ *Comment*

In St Matthew's Gospel we have this wonderful story of the wheat and the tares. Jesus says that the kingdom of heaven may be compared to someone who sowed good seed in his field, but at night the evil one came and sowed tares among the good seed. Tares are difficult to spot until they are fully grown, but then, when they are mature, they can be seen and removed, leaving the corn safe.

Jesus reminds us that this world is made up of good and bad people, and it is not easy to tell which is which sometimes. Sometimes evil masquerades as good, and the other way around. The lesson to be learnt, though, is that it is not we who should make the judgement about those who are good or evil. That judgement is to be left to God. We are simply called to live this life in the best way we can.

However, our newspapers show us that as a nation we continually make judgements about other people, often on very poor foundations. Our press and television encourage us in this habit, but we too are never far behind them. Listen to our conversations, often mere gossip that is hurtful and unkind. There used to be a saying 'If you can't say anything good about someone, then don't say it.' Perhaps as a society we need to remember this saying, and leave judgements to God. At the end of time God, the Great Judge, will judge all people according to how they have lived this life.

PROPER 12

Sunday between 24 July and 30 July

An exploration of the kingdom of heaven is carried out through the parables of the kingdom in St Matthew's Gospel.

Genesis 29.15–28
Romans 8.26–39
Matthew 13.31–33, 44–52

- Bibles
- Texts of the kingdom parables in St Matthew's Gospel.
- Craft items – see list below.

☐ *Starter*

Divide the congregation into small groups and allocate one of the following parables of the kingdom to them. Children may want to work together with some adult help. You may wish to appoint group leaders prior to the service:

Matthew 13.31–32: the mustard seed
Matthew 13.33: yeast
Matthew 13.44: the great treasure
Matthew 13.45–46: fine pearls
Matthew 13.47–50: the dragnet
Matthew 13.51–52: the householder

Allocate Bibles to each group and ask them to read through their parable. Then encourage them to find some way of explaining this parable to other adults, and to children, through:

- a story
- poetry
- a picture or frieze
- drama
- dance

This may mean that they carry out two activities, one for adults and one for children. Note that the group looking at Matthew 13.51–52 may need some extra help! You will also need to encourage each group to start with a time of planning.

Provide as much art and craft material as possible to include:

newspapers
paper
pens/felt-tips
tissue paper
tin foil
glue
scissors
pencils
fabric
frieze paper

☐ *Conclusion*

Listen to and look at as many of the finished explanations as possible. Put up any artwork under the heading 'Parables of the kingdom of heaven'.

☐ *Comment*

Jesus envisages the kingdom of heaven as something that begins secretly and quietly, and as something that has a tiny beginning. Nevertheless it is something that grows swiftly and becomes very large. But all things have to start somewhere and from one person. So God's kingdom is seen as a mustard seed, the smallest of seeds which grows into an enormous tree. Or again, it is seen as leaven (or as we would say, yeast), the small living piece of fermented dough which generates growth in the flour and produces fresh loaves of bread.

Again the kingdom of heaven is like buried treasure or a pearl. It is something so precious that a person would do anything to gain it. Or it is like a dragnet which gathers all fish into its mesh. Only at the harvest when the good and the bad are separated will the worthless be thrown away. This reminds us of the parable of the wheat and tares. It is God who will judge the good and the bad at the end of time.

But what is the kingdom of heaven? Well, it is God's kingdom of love, which is both here and not here. The kingdom is partially present, as we can see from all the good in our world, but it is equally not here completely, as we can see from all the evil around us. Our life's work is to see this wonderful kingdom come fully. As we say every time we say the Lord's Prayer: 'Thy kingdom come'.

☐ *Prayers*
For the coming of God's kingdom.

PROPER 13

Sunday between 31 July and 6 August

We may wonder why we cannot hear God, but in the midst of our noisy lives if we never listen it is hardly surprising.

Genesis 32.22–31
Romans 9.1–5
Matthew 14.13–21

- *Optional:* Someone to speak about retreats.
- Focal points – see list below*.

☐ *Starter*
Talk with the congregation about the need for silence and retreat. You might want to explore the following:

- When did you last spend more than one hour in silence (no radio, TV, or CDs)?
- Do you like being on your own?
- Do you like silence?
- When did you last spend a whole day (or a half a day) on your own?
- Who feels that it is impossible to live without noise, without speech, and without people around?

☐ *Optional*
Ask someone to speak about the benefit of a retreat, and of silence. This might be someone who has recently been on retreat, or it might be someone from a local retreat centre.

□ *Comment*

Jesus must have frequently felt the need for silence and for space. He lived in a very populated part of the world. Israel is only a small country, some 50 miles long by about 25 miles wide with many towns and thousands of people. In our Gospel reading today we see him escaping to the other side of the Sea of Galilee after hearing the news about the death of John the Baptist.

It may be that he felt the need to escape to deal with the news of the death of his cousin, John. Equally it may have been that he just needed to get away from all those people who were following him. Or it may have been that he needed to spend time with God.

Before any major decision or change in his life Jesus always set aside time to be with his heavenly Father. Always he sought to match God's will to his own and to be strengthened for the time ahead. At this point in his life he must have known what was going to lie ahead of him. The death of John could only have confirmed this.

Our lives are often busy and frequently noisy. We too need to find time to be alone with God, and to stop the clamour of our minds. Only when we are still can we hope to hear God's still, small, voice. Only when we are tuned into God can we know the way to go.

□ *Conclusion*

Set up as many focal points as possible and encourage the congregation to go and sit in silence and meditate. Where possible put hassocks or cushions or chairs around the focal points. Any of the following would be suitable:

- One or more traditional pictures, e.g. Christ washing the feet of his disciples, the father welcoming his son back, etc.
- A large cross, with a crown of thorns.
- A large ewer of water, a bowl and a towel.
- Icons.
- Water running into a bowl (the kind usually found in the garden).
- A red piece of cloth, nails and a hammer.
- A chalice and paten, bread and wine.
- An empty crib and a lit candle.
- A banner with a suitable inscription.
- A large candle surrounded by smaller candles.
- A collection of books of religious poetry.

Allow as much time as possible for people to become really silent and to appreciate the space.

* In this service you may need to find a place for young children to 'be silent'.

PROPER 14

Sunday between 7 August and 13 August

The secret of maintaining faith in God is to keep our eyes firmly focused on Jesus.

Genesis 37.1–4, 12–28
Romans 10.5–15
Matthew 14.22–33

- 2 children and their parents (one learning to ride, and one to walk).
- Paper and pencils.
- Bibles.

☐ *Starter*

Invite a child who is just learning to ride a bicycle (but who has not yet learnt) and one of their parents, to show everyone how they are getting on with their riding. Or invite a parent, and their small child who is learning to walk, to help. Alternatively use both.

Encourage the child who is cycling to 'have a go', with the parent holding the back of their seat. Cycle all the way down the aisle with the parent carefully holding the back of the seat. Now try again, this time the parent should let go halfway, the child may well wobble and fall off, especially when they realize the parent is no longer holding the seat. Make sure the child is praised for the attempt, whether they stay on or fall off.

If a parent and small child are helping, show how the toddler walks holding the parent's hand or hands. Now try by holding the child just a little away from the parent. They will probably take one step and fall into the parent's arms, but any further would probably be beyond them.

☐ *Comment*

After the feeding of the five thousand Jesus sends the disciples away, no doubt partly to draw the crowds of people away, but also to give himself some space to be alone with God. So it is that the disciples are on the lake alone without Jesus when the storm brews up. We are told that the 'waves battered the boat' and that they 'were far from land'. The storms on the Sea of Galilee are notoriously fierce, so the disciples may well have been fearful for their lives.

Whatever happened, we know that Jesus was there at the moment when he was needed, although the disciples are terrified by his appearance for he is walking on the water. As usual Peter recovers first and cries impetuously,

> 'Lord, if it is you, command me to come to you on the water.'
> (Matthew 14.28)

He has complete faith that if Christ calls him it would be possible to go to him quite safely across the water. Like a child learning to walk or cycle, Jesus is there to give him the confidence to go on. But like a child when he thinks about it too much, his faith wavers and he needs to be rescued by Jesus. His faith is not yet foolproof.

Our faith can be, all too often, like Peter's. One moment our faith is strong and we do amazing things, but when the going gets rough and we think too much about ourselves, it departs from us and we need rescuing. The secret is to keep our eyes straight ahead fixed on Jesus and not on all that is going on around us. If we know our goal then we shall be steadfast on the path.

 ☐ *Conclusion*

In small groups write about the incident from the Gospel in no more than 12 words, with only one or two words per line. First read through the story again (Matthew 14.22–33). Then as a group decide what is the essence of the story. Exclude the parts of the story that are not as important, before having a go at producing a mini-story.

Come together and listen to all the stories.

PROPER 15

Sunday between 14 August and 20 August

What comes out of our mouths comes out of our heart and soul, so there is a need to think carefully about what we say for it reflects what we feel and believe.

Genesis 45.1–15
Romans 11.1–2a, 29–32
Matthew 15.(10–20), 21–28

- Enid Blyton books.
- 'Janet and John' reading books.
- Historical romance books.
- OHP or flip chart, and pens.

☐ *Starter*

Gather together a large number of books, some old children's reading books (e.g. Janet and John), some traditional children's adventure books of the early part of the last century (e.g. Enid Blyton), and some traditional historical romantic novels. Divide these among the congregation.

Invite the congregation to look through the books for evidence of a 'bygone age'. They are looking for sentences or actions that no longer apply in today's world. Examples might be: the need for a chaperone; a family who has a cook, etc.

Then ask them to search for language that is inappropriate today.

See how many examples can be collected. You might want to put them up on an OHP or flip chart, or simply listen to people's examples.

☐ *Comment*

Jesus laid down principles which is why what he says still applies today. In today's Gospel reading, he is teaching the people. There is obviously a large number of Pharisees present, for we are told that they took offence at his words. The Pharisees were strict Jews who tried to live according to the law of Moses. If this had been all, Jesus would surely have found them to be his greatest allies. Unfortunately too many of them had the 'more than my job's worth' attitude, and their strict adherence to the law meant they were blind to the bigger picture.

For the Pharisee, who tried hard to keep to the letter of the law, what he ate and drank was extremely important. The law that God had given through Moses had laid down exactly what was allowed, and what was forbidden. But here Jesus is telling them that the food laws are unimportant. What really matters is not whether a person eats a forbidden food (e.g. an animal with webbed feet, for instance), for that merely goes through the body and out of it. What does matter is what is in a person's heart, for that can lead to all kinds of evil.

This principle has applications today. For example, as Christians we need to be aware of what we say . For what we say is a small example of what we believe and what we feel. Looking at the kinds of things people used to say in historical books and in children's novels in the past, helps us to see how beliefs have changed. We immediately find some things odd. They don't apply to today any more. For many people today the use of the word 'men' or 'mankind' no longer applies to men *and* women. These phrases are no longer adequate for some when thinking of all people. It isn't just a fad, it's more than that, the use of such phrases is seen as representing a misguided and out-of-date belief. Words are but representations of what we think and what we believe. So today we ask God to help us think about the words we use, and to be honest with ourselves in acknowledging when words represent beliefs that we should reject.

□ *Conclusion*

Continue to explore phrases and sentences that no longer apply. Discuss as a whole congregation what things are no longer acceptable because they reflect ideas that have been rejected, and which would be taking 'political correctness' too far. For example:

- Is asking 'Would you like milk with your coffee' rather than 'Do you want black or white?', preferable? Or is this taking things too far?
- Are phrases like 'good girl' to an older woman acceptable?
- What about the use of the word 'love' to a stranger. Is this acceptable?

□ *Optional*

You could choose to look at inclusive language, if appropriate. For example in many churches the invitation to confession invites 'all men'. Is this appropriate for the twenty-first century, and how do women feel about language that seems to exclude them?

PROPER 16

Sunday between 21 August and 27 August

Jesus established his church and built it on the disciple Peter, the most ordinary of men.

Exodus 1.8—2.10
Romans 12.1–8
Matthew 16.13–20

- Group 1: Bibles, list of Bible readings for all the group, frieze paper, fat pens, art materials for drawing, if desired.
- Group 2: Card, paper, paints or crayons, scissors, possibly A3 paper.
- Group 3: Bibles, large sheets of coloured sugar paper, glue, small garden canes, string, scissors, pencils, instructions for banners
- Group 4: Bibles, A4 sheet of white paper, A4 sheet of black sugar paper, wax crayons, preferably fairly large ones, baby oil, cotton wool, Pritt-Stick, a ruler, a pencil, scissors, and a fat black felt-tip pen.
- Group 5: Bibles and list of readings.
- Group 6: Paper, pencils, copies of the different creeds.
- Group 7: Card, scissors, pencils, copies of haloes, glitter, and paint or crayons.

□ *Starter*

Carry out as many activities as possible which involve finding out about St Peter. For those who may have looked up the life of St Peter in Proper 6, make sure that they join a group that involves something a little different. People can work in small groups or on their own. Appoint leaders for each activity, who can gather all the materials beforehand. Use every possible space in the church, or in any additional rooms.

FINDING OUT ABOUT ST PETER

Group 1

Gather a group of people to look up the following and create a large time-line on frieze paper of St Peter's life. If desired this could be accompanied with sketches of what is discovered.

- What was Peter's early name? (Acts 15.14; 2 Peter 1.1)
- What was his father's name? (Matthew 16.17)
- Where did Peter come from? (John 1.44)
- Who was his brother? (Mark 1.16)
- Who was his brother a disciple of? (John 1.35, 40)
- Was he single or married? (Mark 1.30)
- What else can you find out about his personal life? (1 Corinthians 9.5)
- Where did Peter have a house? (Mark 1.21, 1.29)
- What was wrong with his speech? (Mark 14.70)

Group 2

Read John 1.42, Mark 1.17, 1 Corinthians 1.12, 1 Corinthians 15.5, Galatians 2.9 and Matthew 16.13–19. Then create your own badge for Peter based on what you have learnt. Alternatively a group might like to work *together* to produce a badge or flag for St Peter. Use paint or crayons to produce the badge or flag on the A3 paper.

Group 3

Read John 1.42, Mark 1.17, 1 Corinthians 1.12, 1 Corinthians 15.5, Galatians 2.9 and Matthew 16.13–19. Then in twos or threes create a banner for St Peter based on what you have learnt. Take two large sheets of coloured sugar paper, one piece becomes the body of the banner, and one the top and bottom of the banner. Divide and cut the second sheet into one third and two thirds, fringe the one third and attach to the bottom of the first sheet. Fold the two thirds, cut to look like the top of a castle and put a small cane through it. Attach to the top of the first sheet. Then create your picture out of different coloured sugar paper. Cut out large letters for your banner. Arrange and stick down.

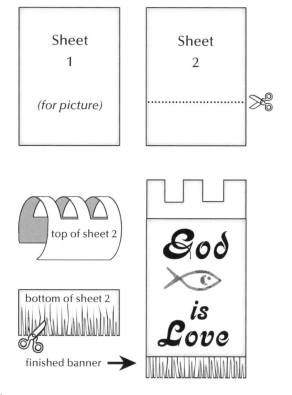

Group 4

Read John 1.42, Mark 1.17, 1 Corinthians 1.12, 1 Corinthians 15.5, Galatians 2.9 and Matthew 16.13–19. Think about what would symbolize St Peter, and then create a stained glass window.

Draw a window shape on the black paper and cut away the
inside part that is the glass window. Put the white paper below
the black window frame and draw round the cut-out part. The
window outline will now be on the white paper. Think about the
picture you are going to draw, and draw this in the window area
of the white paper. Make sure that the picture is thick and
chunky and not too intricate. Take the fat black felt-tip and go
over all the outlines. Divide any big space with the black pen, to
make it look like lead in a window. Use coloured wax crayons to
fill in the different areas of the picture, and leave at least one
blank for white. Finally dip the cotton wool into the baby oil
and wipe it over the wax. When the oil dries it will make it
translucent. Place the black frame over the window and stick it
down. Display the 'stained glass' picture in a window for best
effect.

Group 5

Find out about the controversy in the new church over whether to circumcise the non-Jews who were joining them. What happened? Write up the story in tabloid form on a large sheet of paper to explain to others what the whole issue was about. Look up the following:

- Genesis 17.1-14
- Acts 10
- Acts 11.1–18
- Acts 15.1–21
- Galatians 2.11–14

Group 6

In the creed we say that we believe 'in the communion of saints'.

- What is the 'communion of saints' and do you believe in it?
- What relevance does the 'communion of saints' have for the church?
- Do you think there is a difference between the saints who were apostles and those in subsequent centuries?
- Can you produce arguments for and against inviting the saints to pray for us or with us?
- Is there a prayer that you can write as a group or a couple that refers to a saint or saints, and which you can all feel happy about?

Group 7

As a group have a look at haloes and their different shapes. The leader might provide traditional pictures showing saints with haloes, or if your church has stained glass windows where there are haloes, take a walk round the church to look at them.
Finally create a halo to fit yourself, out of card.

☐ *Conclusion*

Allow everyone time to see the work that has been produced, and to hear back from the groups.

☐ *Comment*

Peter was one of the first disciples to be called by Jesus. Whenever the disciples are mentioned his name is first, and he is always one of the inner circle. Impulsive, loyal and totally human he is the archetype disciple. He makes mistakes, he gets it wrong, but in the end it is he who is the leader of the new church.

His symbols, the fishing net and the keys, are typical of the different sides of this man. He is after all a fisherman, a man with a thick, north-country Galilean accent that even the maids in Jerusalem recognize. He is also the man who will be a fisher of men and who will spread the good news of the gospel wherever he goes. It was also to Peter that Jesus gave the keys of heaven. Those whom he forgave would be forgiven in heaven. He is the rock on which Jesus built his church.

Before the resurrection Peter falls in and out of trouble; he fails to recognize what is happening at the Transfiguration and makes inappropriate statements; his faith fails him when Jesus calls him to walk across the lake to him; and ultimately in Jerusalem he denies Jesus three times. But after Pentecost we see a totally new man. He faces the authorities and proclaims Jesus as the risen Lord; together with John he heals the lame man at the temple gates; and he finally overcomes all his ingrained traditional training and welcomes gentiles into the new church.

God can, and does, take ordinary men and women, who offer themselves wholeheartedly to his service, and he produces saints.

PROPER 17

Sunday between 28 August and 3 September

We need to keep our eyes ahead on the vision which is part of the bigger picture for the church.

Exodus 3.1–15
Romans 12.9–21
Matthew 16.21–28

- A large number of mission statements.
- Large sheets of paper and fat pens.
- OHP or flip chart and fat pen.

☐ *Starter*

Before the service gather together as many mission statements as possible, e.g. statements made by big companies of what they intend to do for the company and their customers, from charities, from the diocese, or from other churches. Most secular companies now create mission statements to explain where they are going and what they are about, so try to gather as many as possible.

Photocopy some of the mission statements onto OHP transparencies, or write the gist of them onto large sheets of paper and put onto a flip chart. Alternatively make as many copies as possible and pass round the congregation. Either discuss the mission statements with everyone, or allow people to discuss them with their neighbours.

- What do they mean?
- What do they promise the customer or shareholder?
- How appropriate are they?
- Do you think the company or group are managing to fulfil their mission statement?

☐ *Optional*

If your church has a mission statement you might like to take this opportunity to look at it again.

- How appropriate is it now?
- How far is the church fulfilling its mission statement?
- Would the congregation want to change anything?

- Do you want to recommend to the Church Council that it is time to look at it in depth again with a view to revising it?

☐ *Comment*

As we can see from the Gospel reading, Peter sometimes gets it wrong. He is a very ordinary man and sometimes he misses the point entirely. Jesus begins to prepare the disciples for what is to happen to him. He has been trying to do this for some time, but they have stubbornly refused to hear him. Now he is more direct. Matthew says:

> Jesus began to show his disciples that he must go to Jerusalem and undergo great suffering at the hands of the elders and chief priests and scribes, and be killed, and on the third day be raised. (Matthew 16.21)

Peter only sees the first section of the sentence: Jesus is to suffer and be killed! He is so taken up with the fact that his beloved Lord is to suffer that he cannot see beyond this. He ignores the last phrase, that Jesus will be raised on the third day.

It is the natural response of anyone to a loved one's news that they are to die. We try to do everything to keep them back, even though the loved one's mind is set on higher things beyond our recognition. It is wrong when it happens to our loved ones, and it was wrong when Peter tried to hold Jesus back. For Jesus had his mind set on the bigger picture. He knew that he was going to be with his Father and that he was coming to the end of his work here on earth. That is not to denigrate the dreadful time he was to go through, but it is to remind us that Jesus always had his mind set on the bigger world picture.

In our church life all too often we are like Peter. We can only see the here and now. We don't want to change what exists now; we don't want to move into the future because it might be too uncomfortable. Mission statements are a company's or church's way of looking into the future. They keep our eyes on the future and on the wider picture, taking us out of our comfortable, insular pew and reminding us of the bigger needs. We rarely, if ever, achieve everything in a mission statement, indeed if we did it would need revising. Mission statements are things to work on and to nibble away at, so that we continually move forward.

☐ *Conclusion*

Whether or not your church has a mission statement, gather in small groups to design a plan for your church community. Give each group one or more large sheets of paper and fat pens. Put up the following on an OHP or flip chart, or produce copies for each group. Children might like to work together with a leader.

- Imagine your church community in 30 years, what would you like to see?
- Now design what needs to happen in your church in 20 years' time, in ten years' time and in five years' time. Keep the planning loose, headings rather than fully thought-out plans.
- What one thing would you do in the next six months to make a start on your plan?

Finally, hear back from all the groups, and hang their work up so that everyone can see it. Remember that the children will be the adults running this church in 30 years' time (if you have managed to keep them!). You might want to take their thoughts very seriously.

PROPER 18

Sunday between 4 September and 10 September

Jesus said that where two or three are gathered in his name, he is there among them. This week looks at different kinds of prayers and praying.

Exodus 12.1–14
Romans 13.8–14
Matthew 18.15–20

- Group 1: Children's prayer books, paper and pens or pencils.
- Group 2: Possibly books of intercessions, paper and pens or pencils.
- Group 3: Newspapers, possibly paper and pens or pencils.
- Group 4: Paper and pens or pencils, possibly books of resource material for ideas.
- Group 5: Bibles, possibly paper and pens or pencils.
- Group 6: Flat, smooth stones, enamel paint. Brushes, PVA glue, examples of Christian symbols or other resource material.
- Group 7: Candles, possibly of various shapes and sizes, paper and pens or pencils.
- Group 8: Magazines and newspapers, possibly glue and large sheet(s) of paper, alternatively, paper and pens or pencils.

☐ *Starter*

Establish as many groups as possible to look at prayer. You might wish to create one or two focal places for silent prayer (see Proper 13 for ideas). Most groups will need leaders. Use as many of the following ideas as desired:

Group 1 (of adults)
Gather a number of children's prayer books and look at them. What do you like or dislike about them? What subjects appear to be missing? Would you say language and concepts are appropriate? Try writing some prayers for children, on the following subjects:
- night-time
- meal-time
- for the sick or dying
- intercessions

Perhaps these could be tidied up or finished later and made into a booklet for use by the children.

Group 2
Provide training for intercessions. Invite a number of people who have never led the intercessions in church, to join this group. Give them some basic training in leading the intercessions, and encourage them to try their hand at writing some intercessions.

Group 3
Create prayers for the day. Provide this group with a large number of newspapers, current or out-of-date. Invite them to look through them, imagining the paper is that day's. Encourage them to find subjects for daily prayer by asking them to find:
- two things for which they wish to thank God.
- two things which remind them of something they wish to ask God for *personal* forgiveness.
- two things in the *world* for which they wish to ask God's forgiveness.
- two things for which they wish to ask God's help.

Suggest that the group could use this technique to pray, each day.

Group 4
Create prayer diaries. Discuss what a prayer diary might be, and how it might be used. What would they put in it, e.g. pictures, sayings, thoughts, articles? When would they use it? How often would they want to review the diary? Could this be done with another person, e.g. each have their own diary, but periodically review the results? Start the first page of the prayer diary.

Group 5

Carry out some Bible study followed by prayer. Read through the Gospel reading for today (Matthew 18.15–20) and discuss its implications as a group. Then discuss how the passage might be used for personal prayer. What subjects might be brought up for prayer? As a group now use the subjects discussed for group prayer, or allow each person to pray in silence.

Group 6

Make some prayer stones. Each member of the group will need a large, flat, smooth stone. They will also need small tins of enamel paint and PVA glue and brushes. Talk with the group about silent meditation and the need for a focal point. Look at some examples of simple religious artwork. Then encourage everyone to paint a simple religious symbol onto their stone. When it is dry cover with PVA glue. This will give a shine to the stone. Even though the stones may not be finished, or dry, make sure they are used for a few moments for silent meditation in this service.

Group 7

Carry out a candle meditation. Create a focal point using candles. This could be one large candle, like a paschal candle, or different shapes and sizes of candles. Give each person a piece of paper and a pen or pencil. Invite them to be silent and to meditate on the candles for a few minutes. When they feel ready they are to jot down words and phrases that occur to them as a result of looking at the candles. If desired, they might want to create a simple two-line prayer inspired by the candles.

Group 8

Write, and burn, confessions for the world and for yourself. Provide a large number of newspapers or magazines for the group. Encourage the group to look at them to start a list of 'confessions for the world'. The group should make the list together, either by writing out the subjects onto a small piece of paper, or by cutting out the headlines and sticking them onto a large sheet of paper. The group might also like to work as individuals after this and to create their own personal confession list. Finally go outside and burn the confessions in a large galvanized bucket or other suitable container.

□   *Comment*

Jesus says that 'where two or three are gathered in my name, I am there among them' (Matthew 18.20), and again that 'if two of you agree on earth about anything you ask, it will be done for you by my Father in heaven' (Matthew 18.19). He gives us tremendous power, but in a way it comes with a warning. It is not up to us to ask for ridiculous things: 'Can I win the lottery?' or 'I would like a red bike for my birthday'. Prayers are to be used sensibly, almost always for the good of others and the wider community. We may pray for ourselves, but *our* needs are not as important as others.

We are also reminded that when we come together as a church community, Jesus is with us. We come into the presence of the living Lord, and it doesn't mean that we have to be specially quiet or put on a ridiculously solemn face. On the contrary, Jesus was just as much at home at a wedding as he was in the temple. But it does mean that we need to leave our selfishness, our prejudices, and our pride behind.

Prayer should be the backbone of our lives as Christians. It should be as natural as breathing. We should live our lives in a state of prayer, as it were, so that it weaves in and out of our daily lives. We don't need special language or attitudes, we just need space, quiet and a knowledge of what is happening in our world and community. How can we pray if we don't know what is happening around us? How can we pray if we never find time to be alone with God? How can we pray if we only think about ourselves?

□ *Conclusion*

Hear back from all the groups and look at, or listen to, their work. Put up any work and leave for some weeks. Remember to ask in the future about those who started prayer diaries, or who started to produce the children's book of prayers. Encourage those who wrote the intercessions to try their hand at them in public worship, where appropriate.

□ *Prayer*

Have some silent prayer in this service, or a guided meditation. If suitable, use some of the prayers that have been produced today.

PROPER 19
Sunday between 11 September and 17 September

Christians need to dissociate themselves from the 'blame and gain' culture and learn true forgiveness.

Exodus 14.19–31
Romans 14.1–12
Matthew 18.21–35

- Newspapers and magazines.
- A large roll of frieze paper or an old roll of wallpaper (use the back).
- Glue.
- Forgive Me sheets for all the congregation.
- Pens or pencils.
- *Optional:* A galvanized bucket and matches to burn the sheets during the words of the Peace.

☐ *Starter*

Gather a large number of magazines and newspapers (preferably of many different dates) and give them out to the congregation. Their task is to look for examples of incidents where people are unable to forgive someone else, and cut them out. Some may well be duplicates, but this is not too important.

Now employ any children or teenagers to unroll some frieze paper or wallpaper and stick the stories onto the back of the paper. They could at this stage, if they want, remove some of the duplicate stories.

Create a large heading of 'Unable to forgive' and put up friezes somewhere in the church.

☐ *Optional*

Invite someone to talk about how hard it is to forgive.

☐ *Comment*

In the Lord's Prayer we say 'forgive us our sins as we forgive those who sin against us', but it is fairly obvious from looking at these newspapers that we find it a little difficult to carry out this petition. All too often we don't see our own sins. We only see the sins of others.

Jesus says that we should forgive others 'seventy-seven times', and proceeds to tell the story of the king and the unjust slave. Despite the size of his debt the slave is forgiven and his family are saved from being sold. Yet the moment the king's back is turned the slave in turn throws one of his debtors into prison, and rightly his fellow-slaves are appalled. The king in his turn reacts with anger and hands the slave over to be tortured, so the end result is far worse for the unjust slave.

In our society we have a 'blame and gain' culture. If something goes wrong there is no such thing as an accident, no such thing as our fault, and no such thing as forgiveness. We need to know whom to blame and whom to sue. Indeed professionals advertise on our television that if someone is to blame they will make sure that you can sue them and gain something from the incident.

It might seem to be ridiculously naive to forgive someone again and again, but the Christian should remember that God forgives us again and again, even up to seventy-seven times!

☐ *Conclusion*
Before the service produce small cards for every member of the congregation, as follows.

~ *Forgive me!* ~

Lord God, I ask your forgiveness for not forgiving

Joan who did not return my book

Give out the cards and pens or pencils, and invite everyone to be as hard as possible on themselves. If they feel the slightest grudge or lack of enthusiasm towards anyone they should be encouraged to write the circumstances down.

Gather up the sheets of paper and take them outside and burn them. Alternatively encourage people to go home and burn them.

☐ *Optional*
Close with the words of the Peace:

Leader   The Lord be with you.
All   And also with you.

Everyone shares a sign of peace, a handshake or a kiss.

PROPER 20

Sunday between 18 September and 24 September

God welcomes all who come to him. Those who come last will be as welcome as those who come first.

Exodus 16.2–15
Philippians 1.21–30
Matthew 20.1–16

- Speakers who will talk about how they came to faith
- Group 1:   Old greeting cards, coloured or white card, scissors, glue, list of suitable verses (e.g. Lamentations 3.33; Isaiah 30.15a; Psalm 103.8; Ezekiel 34.23; Joel 2.13; Nahum 1.7).
- Group 2:   White card, a number of sheets of wrapping paper with a small repeating pattern, scissors, glue, Pritt-Tabs or Pritt-Tak or Sellotape, and suitable Bible verses (see Group 1).
- Group 3:   White card, scissors, pencils, and suitable Bible verses (see Group 1).
- Group 4:   White card, scissors, pencils, glue, coloured tissue paper, and suitable Bible verses (see Group 1).
- Group 5:   White paper, black sugar paper, wax crayons (preferably fairly large ones), baby oil, cotton wool, glue, a ruler, a pencil, scissors, and a fat black felt-tip pen.

☐ *Starter*

Invite two or three people to come and speak about how they came
to faith. Try to find someone who came to faith when they were
very young and who might now be in their middle or late years;
someone who came to faith in their thirties or forties and who may
be older now; and someone who is elderly but who came to faith
late in life.

Ask the speakers to talk of how old they were when they came to
faith, and how or why it occurred. In other words what led them to
become a Christian and a member of the faith community?

You may wish to interview them, rather than let them just talk.

☐ *Comment*

The Gospel reading for today is the story of the labourers in the
vineyard. The harvesting of the vines was always a difficult time for
vineyard owners, for the weather was likely to break at any
moment. If the rains came, the crop would be ruined. Early in the
day, the owner contracts to employ some labourers to work in his
vineyard, and later he returns to the village square to employ more
workers. Finally, near the end of the day with the crop still not in,
he employs the last group of men still hoping for employment.

All of this is fine until the reckoning comes. Then the owner pays
all the men the same amount, even those who have worked through
the heat of the day. Those who came in last receive the same
amount as those who have done a full day's work. This seems unfair
to those who agreed to work first thing in the morning and they
complain. The owner points out that they should not complain if he
chooses to be generous.

This is another parable about the kingdom of heaven. Jesus is
saying that whether we become a Christian in our childhood, in our
maturity, or even on our deathbed when we are elderly, God will
welcome us as one of his treasured children. We get no more special
status if we have worked for him all our lives, or if we have only just
come to faith at the last moment. Of course that is no good reason
for leaving our conversion to the last moment, we may not get the
chance!

The point is that our heavenly Father loves us and welcomes us
whenever we turn to him. Of his great love he offers us equality
whenever we choose to turn to him.

☐ *Conclusion*

Create 'God loves you cards' to deliver to as many people as
possible whom you feel may need God's love and your prayers at
this time. Create the cards in groups and while they are being made
talk about different ways in which God's love could be taken to
other people.

Group 1

Create cards. Provide as many pictures from old greetings cards as possible, coloured or white card, scissors, glue, and one or two suitable verses (e.g. Lamentations 3.33; Isaiah 30.15a; Psalm 103.8; Ezekiel 34.23; Joel 2.13; Nahum 1.7). Make cards and write one of the verses inside the card. Deliver to someone you know who is in need, and sign it yourself.

Group 2

Make decoupage cards. You will need white card, and a number of sheets of wrapping paper with a small repeating pattern. Cut and fold the card. Cover the front of the card with the wrapping paper and stick it down. Then cut out a flower or part of the small repeating pattern, two or three times. Put a small piece of Pritt-Tak, Pritt-Tab, or folded Sellotape onto the centre of the small flower on the card. Attach the same flower, and repeat. Part of the pattern will now stand out in a three-dimensional way. Inside the card write a Bible verse (see Group 1) and sign. Deliver to someone you know who is in need.

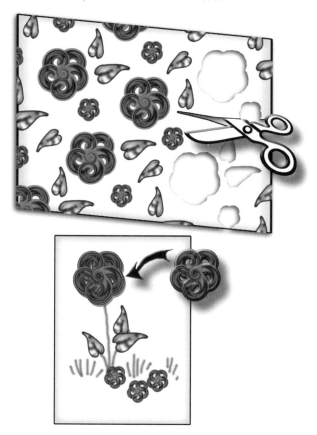

Group 3

Make praying hand cards. Take a sheet of A4 card and fold it across the width in half. Now put your hand down on the paper, with fingers together and the little figure lined up along the fold. Draw round your hand and cut out the shape, leaving the fold uncut. Inside the card write a Bible verse (see Group 1) and sign. Deliver to someone you know who is in need.

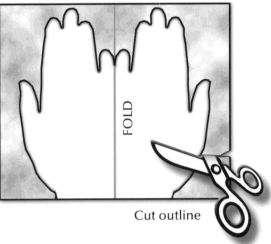

Cut outline

Group 4

Make butterfly cards. Cut and fold the card. Draw half of a large butterfly shape and cut round it, so making the card a butterfly shape. Then taking minute pieces of coloured tissue paper (yellows and reds predominantly) screw them up and stick them onto the outline of the butterfly. Inside the card write a Bible

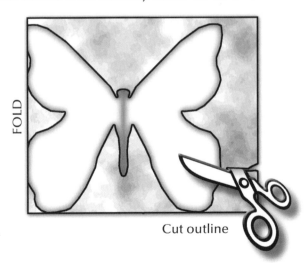

Cut outline

verse (see Group 1) and sign. Before delivering to someone you know who is in need shake upside down to check if the tissue paper is firmly stuck down.

Group 5
Make a stained glass picture to go into a card. You will need white paper, black sugar paper, wax crayons (preferably fairly large ones), baby oil, cotton wool, glue, a ruler, a pencil, scissors, and a fat black felt-tip pen. Draw a window shape on the black paper and cut away the inside part that is the glass window. Put the white paper below the black window frame and draw round the cut-out part. The window outline will now be on the white paper. Now think about the picture you are going to draw (perhaps a cross, or a fish symbol) and draw this in the window area of the white paper. Make sure that the picture is thick and chunky and not too intricate. Take the fat black felt-tip and go over all the outlines. Any big space needs to be divided with the black pen, to make it look like lead in a window. Use coloured wax crayons to fill in the areas of the picture and leave at least one blank for white. Finally dip the cotton wool into the baby oil and wipe it over the wax. When the oil dries it will make it translucent. Place the black frame over the window and stick it down. Now place the 'stained glass' picture loosely into a piece of folded white card. You might want to cut a frame inside the front page of the white card so that the 'stained glass' can be seen through it, before the person to whom you are giving it takes it out and hangs it up at a window. Inside the card write a Bible verse (see Group 1) and sign. Deliver to someone you know who is in need.

□ *Prayer*
Pray for all new Christians and for those who will visit others in the neighbourhood with their cards.

PROPER 21

Sunday between 25 September and 1 October

God wants action not words. He wants us to live our lives, following his commands. It is not enough simply to sound like a Christian, we must follow this through into the way we live.

Exodus 17.1–7
Philippians 2.1–13
Matthew 21.23–32

- Script for the guided meditation.
- Copies for the questions after the meditation (or an OHP or flip chart could be used).

 ☐ *Starter*

Carry out some guided meditation. Encourage everyone to sit as comfortably as they can, legs uncrossed, hands perhaps loose at their side or in their lap. If the congregation are not used to guided meditation it may be wise to talk about some ground rules first. You might use some of the following.

GUIDED MEDITATION

- Ensure that everyone is as relaxed as possible.
- Ensure that the church is warm.
- Offer a large focal point if desired.
- Invite everyone to enter the story and to use their imagination.
- Carry out a stilling exercise if desired (relax the feet, then the ankles, then the legs, etc.), but this is time-consuming.
- Read slowly and leave space for minds to clothe the ideas with thoughts.
- Encourage everyone to put distracting thoughts to one side when they occur and try to immerse themselves in the storyline again.

Once everyone is relaxed read the storyline fairly slowly in a clear but calm voice, allowing long pauses where the dots appear. If you have never read a guided meditation before practise with one or two people beforehand so they can tell you whether you are reading too quickly or too slowly.

Before starting this story, organize the congregation into groups of three and invite each person in the group to become one of the three people in the story: e.g. the father, the elder son, or the younger son. They are to see the story only through the eyes of their particular character.

THE TWO SONS: A MODERN STORY

There was a father................................
are you that father................................?
Now the father had two sons...
one, the elder was named John, are you that son..............?
and the younger was named Stephen, are you that son..............?

Now the two sons were very different from one another. John, the elder, was a tear-away.......................
always up to mischief...............
Can you see him out late with his friends at the disco..............?
Waking the household up when he comes in late.....................?

The younger son, Stephen, was quieter and well-behaved.................
He helped his mother to carry in the heavy logs for the fire..................
Can you see him at home reading............................?
or on his computer...................................?

Now the father owned a vineyard................................
It was a very profitable vineyard and produced some good wine.......................
All summer this particular year the sun shone on his grapes.............................
and by the time autumn came the grapes were hanging heavy on the vines................

As the autumn approached the father was keen to get his grapes harvested before the weather changed..................................
He looked anxiously at the sky, hoping the rain would stay away...................
Stephen noticed his concern and tried to cheer him up..............................
John shrugged his shoulders, it was always like this, his father worrying as the time came to harvest the grapes.........................

Finally the grapes were ripe and the father came to John and asked him to help with the harvesting.............................

'No way,' said John, on his way out of the door, 'I've arranged to be in town this morning'............

The father was disappointed......................

How was he to get the harvest in on his own?...........................

He approached his younger son, Stephen, and asked him to help with the harvesting.........................

'OK,' agreed Stephen, smiling. 'I'll be with you in a moment'...................

The father went out into the vineyard and started work..........................

The sun shone and it was very hot..................................

The hours went by and still there was no sign of Stephen.............................

The father looked worriedly at the sky............................

Would the rain hold off till tomorrow?...........................

How would he get the grapes harvested with no help?...........

Later in the morning as the father stood up, easing his aching back, he noticed someone coming down the long rows of vines towards him......................

It was John..............................

'Sorry, Dad,' said the elder boy, 'I changed my mind. I can always go to town tomorrow', and he picked up a basket and began to pick the grapes..........................

The father smiled, both relieved and pleased to see him..............................

Now they would surely get the grapes harvested...........................

and the two men steadily worked their way along the rows of grapes....................

Back at the house, Stephen looked up from his computer...........................

He glanced out of the window.........................

He could see his father and John working side by side............................

'Oh, that's all right,' he thought, and went back to his game.....................

Invite the congregation to come slowly back to the present, and give them a moment or two to orientate themselves.

□ *Conclusion*

Working in the groups already set up, discuss the story as told in
the guided meditation. Ask yourselves the following questions:

> - How do I feel about my two sons?/How do I feel about my
>   father?/How do I feel about my brother?
> - What do I want to say to my sons about the time of harvest?/
>   What do I want to say to my father about the time of
>   harvest?
> - How do I feel when no one turns up to help me harvest?/How
>   do I feel about being asked to help with the harvest when I
>   have other plans?
> - How do I feel when John turns up to help?/How do I feel
>   about working with my father?/How do I feel when I see John
>   and my father at work?

□ *Comment*

Jesus uses the parable of the two sons (or the parable of the
vineyard) to tell those who are against him, notably the chief priests
and the Pharisees, a home truth. The meaning is very clear. The
chief priests and the Pharisees are those who have said they will
obey their heavenly Father. Their faith, and the observances of
their religious life are very important to them. They are the son,
who promises to help the father in the vineyard, but who does not
turn up.

The tax collectors, the outcasts, the sick and the rejected, who for
most Jews are deemed to lie outside God's care, they are the son
who refuses to help the father in the vineyard, but who in the end
turns up to help.

Neither son can be said to be the perfect son. The Pharisees
promise all, but do not live up to their faith; the outcasts scorn God
but in the end return to him. Neither offers a wholehearted loving
response to God.

Of course the other way of applying this parable is to ourselves.
The Pharisees are those who profess to be Christians, but their lives
do not match up to what they profess. These Christians look down
on others who do not observe Lent, or attend a Bible study class,
but somehow their faith is not carried into their lives. The outcasts
are those who reject the church and who have no interest in it, yet
these people in the end often live more Christian lives than many
who profess to a faith and in the end many do come back to God.

PROPER 22

Sunday between 2 October and 8 October

Jesus warns the Pharisees, and he warns us, that if we reject him we reject the one who will be our judge one day.

Exodus 20.1–4, 7–9, 12–20
Philippians 3.4b–14
Matthew 21.33–46

- Brick patterns printed onto cards.
- Scissors.
- Pens or pencils.
- Glue.

□ *Starter*
The task today is to make a 'wall'. Before the service print the brick pattern in Appendix A onto card. You will need to draw your own template from the pattern and scale it up to the size shown.
Produce sufficient copies so the congregation can have one each.

First, though, encourage the congregation to work with those either side of them to decide the following:

- Two or three things which show that Jesus is Lord of our lives.
- Two or three things which we might do (or have done) that show how we reject Jesus.

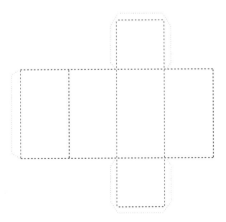

Now give the cards out to everyone in the congregation, also a pencil, scissors and glue. Their task is to make a wall out of 'bricks'. Adults will have to help small children, and children's scissors might be needed.

INSTRUCTIONS FOR MAKING THE BRICKS

- Cut out the brick.
- Score with the back of the scissors all those lines which have to be folded.
- Fold the lines.
- Make into a box.
- Stick down the flaps.

When the bricks are made up write the two positive things that were discovered about Jesus in their life on one side of the brick, and the two negative on the other side of the brick.

□ *Comment*

St Matthew continues to show Jesus campaigning against the chief priests and the Pharisees. The chief priests and the Pharisees are constantly on the watch to try and trip him up, knowing that much of what he says is aimed at them. Finally, he warns them against rejecting the stone which becomes the corner stone that holds the whole building up.

The Jewish religious authorities, the very people that seek to destroy him, are the ones who are most urgently searching for the Messiah who will save their people. This saviour or king to be sent from God is, they know, their only hope. Yet such is their blindness that they entirely fail to see that he is before their very noses, and they reject Jesus. Jesus knows that in their turn they will face his judgement; the man they have rejected will become their judge.

□ *Conclusion*

Now working together in twos create a list of people who reject God's offer of salvation, today. This might be individuals (in which case simply put down Christian names) or it might be whole groups, e.g. those who look for personal satisfaction; drug dealers, etc. Write these onto the bricks, on either end, and build into a wall. One side of the wall could be positive and one negative. Leave the wall in church, for a while, if possible.

PROPER 23
Sunday between 9 October and 15 October

God invites us into his kingdom. Will we accept or reject his invitation?

Exodus 32.1–14
Philippians 4.1–9
Matthew 22.1–14

- A 'script' for the role play and a rehearsal.
- Three main actors, and six more (last scene only).
- Flip chart and fat pen, or OHP and transparency.

☐ *Starter*
Prepare a fairly lengthy role play. This will need some rehearsal beforehand. Read the Gospel for the day *after* the role play. You will need the following characters:

Mr Brown
Mrs Brown
Jennifer Brown (aged 12 years)
Six adults (who only appear in the last scene)

ROLE PLAY

Setting the scene
Mrs and Mrs Jones have a much-loved daughter, Jennifer. The parents have been too busy in the past (both work very hard) to give a birthday party for their daughter. However, this year they have decided they ought to do something because it is her eleventh birthday and soon she will be going to high school.

As each scene opens have someone else enter across the 'stage' with a plaque saying 'Scene 1', 'Scene 2', etc.

Scene 1
Six weeks before Jennifer's birthday
Mr and Mrs Jones and Jennifer begin to plan for the party. Should they do the cooking themselves and have burgers or pizza, or should they have the party at the swimming pool or bowling alley? Perhaps Jennifer wants somewhere even more

exotic! In the end they settle for a buffet at home followed by bowling. Next, the list of those to be invited is carefully thought through. Should they ask X or Y? Perhaps Jennifer wants more to attend than her parents want. Finally, however, the major decisions are made.

Scene 2
Two weeks later

The invitations have been sent out and now the answers are coming in. Mrs Jones enters, bringing a handful of letters. She and Jennifer open them and then comment on who has decided to come. Is there anyone that says 'no' or do they all wish to attend? Jennifer is particularly happy because her two best friends and the boy she is rather keen on have said they will be attending. Mr Jones enters and is told all the good news.

Scene 3
The day of the party

Jennifer enters to ask her mother what she thinks about the clothes she is going to wear 'tonight'. Perhaps they have an argument over the clothes, or perhaps mother suggests wearing something else. Finally, however, things are sorted. Father enters and there is a discussion over the food or the place they are going to and transport.

Scene 4
Half-an-hour before the party

The phone rings and Jennifer answers it. It is her best friend . . . She can't attend the party as her aunt from Scotland has just arrived and she won't be staying very long. Jennifer is upset, but her mother consoles her, after all plenty more people will be coming. Just then Mr Jones enters with two letters for Jennifer. She is excited, thinking they are birthday cards from friends. Instead they turn out to be letters giving excuses why the friends cannot come to the party. One is from the boy she rather likes. There is a knock at the door and Mrs Jones goes out to answer it, returning rather worriedly to say that neither of their neighbours can attend the party. Jennifer has a temper tantrum and storms out saying she never wants another birthday party, and it wasn't her idea anyway.

Scene 5
The party should have started

Mrs Jones is calling upstairs to Jennifer asking her to come downstairs, because someone will surely come to the party any minute, even if they should have arrived half-an-hour ago. Muffled answers from Jennifer. The door opens and in comes Mr Jones with a half-a-dozen people he has gathered on the way home. All know Jennifer slightly – neighbours, the woman from the corner shop, etc. He has invited them to come and join the party. Jennifer comes down stairs, not sure, but discovers that everyone is having a wonderful time, eating and drinking. All of them have been bowling before and are looking forward to joining Jennifer for the evening. They toast Jennifer and wish her luck. Jennifer ends up having a wonderful time and says so at the end, perhaps ending with 'I can't wait for next year's birthday'. Parents smile/collapse in exhaustion.

□ Comment

Our role play has been a modern retelling of the parable of the king and the wedding banquet, but perhaps it has helped us to see how disappointed the king and his son (or in this case Mr and Mrs Jones and Jennifer) must have been. It was the custom to send out the wedding invitations well in advance, although the time was not necessarily included. Everyone had accepted the invitation, and all it needed was for the time to be sent to the guests. This is when the trouble starts. For the guests refuse to attend the wedding banquet, and abuse the king's servants.

There must have been no doubt in the Pharisees' minds that they were under attack by Jesus yet again. For the guests who were invited long ago were the Jews, and when the times draws near they refuse to come. This is almost unimaginable, for all their history has been leading to this point. Imagine how God must have felt, that his chosen people were refusing him yet again. But all is not lost, for the king's servants go and invite anyone they can find in to the feast. So instead of Jews, the gentile world go to the wedding feast.

This parable, and our role play, remind us that we too have been invited to this joyful feast. God offers us, out of love, a place in his kingdom. We turn it down at our peril.

□ Conclusion

Explore with the congregation times when we refuse God's invitation to come in to the feast. Invite them to turn to their neighbour and find two occasions between them when they have felt that they have said 'no' to God.

After a few moments bring the whole congregation together. If possible begin to gather some of these ideas and put them onto a flip chart or OHP. Some people won't want to speak, but allow those who are willing to offer some suggestions.

PROPER 24

Sunday between 16 October and 22 October

We have a dual membership in life – we are members of the country where we live, and we are members of the kingdom of God. We owe allegiance to both.

Exodus 33.12–23
1 Thessalonians 1.1–10
Matthew 22.15–22

- Owing Allegiance forms for everyone, or alternatively a large version.
- A flip chart or OHP.
- Pens or pencils.

□ *Starter*

Create a large board headed 'Owing Allegiance'. The board should look something like the following illustration:

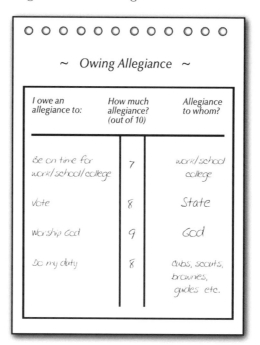

You might wish to start by giving everyone an individual form and asking them to work either on their own, or in twos, to see what they produce, and then collectively work on making up the large board. Alternatively, work on the large board together from the beginning. Encourage people to look at different aspects of their lives, and to be honest about how much allegiance they think they owe. There will obviously be some differences on the ratings. Look at both secular and sacred allegiances, and especially at controversial allegiances.

□ *Comment*

The Pharisees and the Herodians (supporters of Herod) finally mount a united assault upon Jesus. This in itself shows their concern over Jesus, for the two groups mutually loathed each other under normal circumstances. They must have imagined they had Jesus exactly where they wanted him, for whatever he answered to the question, 'Is it lawful to pay taxes to the emperor or not?', he would stand condemned.

To the Jewish nation the thought of an emperor was anathema. Only God was King and only he could demand taxes. They were not prepared to cede that kind of authority to a Roman emperor. The particular tax that the Pharisees and Herodians are speaking about is the tax that every Jewish man and woman had to pay to the government, and if Jesus refuses to recognize the emperor's authority then he would probably be arrested for sedition. Not only this, but Jews were accustomed to paying temple tax until the temple was destroyed in AD 70. After this, possibly around the time that Matthew was writing his Gospel, the Romans attempted to collect the temple tax for the temple of Jupiter in Rome. Of course if Jesus recognized the emperor's authority to collect tax then he was putting himself in the wrong with his own people. He was in an impossible dilemma.

But as always, Jesus pronounces principles, which is why we still find what he had to say so useful today. He takes a small coin and asks whose head is on it. 'The emperor' comes back the answer. 'Give therefore to the emperor the things that are the emperor's, and to God the things that are God's.' Each of us has a dual membership in this life. We belong to God and we belong to a country. We owe our allegiance to both. If, of course, the two clash at some point, then after serious thought and prayer we should trust our allegiance to God. Eric Liddell, the runner in the film *Chariots of Fire*, is forced to make just such a choice when he is expected to run an Olympic qualifying race on a Sunday. He chooses God's wishes in this case over that of his running and therefore over that of his country.

☐   *Conclusion*

In twos, or as a whole congregation, discuss times when allegiances
have been stretched and when duty has been difficult. Look at any
of the following:

- I couldn't get out of bed to go to church.
- I didn't think it would matter if I took a few hours off work, no
  one would notice.
- I added a little extra onto my expenses, no one will know.
- I just couldn't be bothered to turn up for .... (women's group,
  club, etc), they could manage without me this time.
- .... ?

Encourage people to be as honest as possible and to look at
situations objectively.

☐   *Prayer*

Close with a prayer offering God 'our whole allegiance'.

PROPER 25

Sunday between 23 and 29 October inclusive

Deuteronomy 34.1–12
1 Thessalonians 2.1–8
Matthew 22.34–46

- OHP or flip chart and pen.
- Different categories on the OHP or flip chart.
- Storylines for everyone.
- *Optional:* Large sheet of paper and fat pen for the children.

Divide the congregation up into small groups of between four and
six people. Children might like to work together. Spend a few
moments discussing what it might mean to 'love the Lord your God
with all your heart, and with all your soul, and with all your mind'
(and 'with all your strength' as we read elsewhere).

Now put up the following phrases onto an OHP or flip chart, and
explore what it means to love God in the following circumstances:

- At church
- In the family
- At work
- At play
- In our country
- At school
- In our world

Encourage each group to think of at least two practical examples that would show how they might love God. Write these up onto large sheets of paper, with a fat pen. Groups may come up with more than two suggestions, and these could also be listed.

Gather all the suggestions. Ask someone from each group to speak about their suggestions.

□ *Comment*

Jesus' answers were always tailored to the circumstances. He is asked the following by the Pharisees in his audience:

> 'Teacher, which commandment in the law is the greatest?' (Matthew 22.36)

This is no simple question, for to the Pharisees the law of Moses was the essence of their being. Pharisees dedicated their whole life to trying to keep to the law. They worried over whether they would by accident break the law. What did it mean, for instance, not to work on the sabbath? It was the scribes' job to dictate what each action might mean, but it was the Pharisees who tried to obey the entire letter of the law.

Jesus replies:

> 'You shall love the Lord your God with all your heart, and with all your soul, and with all your mind.' (Matthew 22.37)

This is the greatest of all the commandments. We are to love God with every fibre of our being. All our loyalty and all our allegiance is to be given to him. Everything else in life – our families, our friends, and our ambitions – are all to come second place. This is a hard commandment, but nevertheless it is one that we should not flinch from. God must be first in our lives.

However, Jesus follows the Great Commandment with another. The second, he says, is like it:

> 'You shall love your neighbour as yourself.' (Matthew 22.39)

These two are the basis of all God's laws. If we obey these two laws then we shall be living the kind of life that God wants us to live. God's kingdom of love will be brought in when we love God first and love others as much as we love ourselves.

☐ *Conclusion*

Working in small groups look at the following storylines. Encourage everyone to be as selfish as they like and to think of the solutions only from their own perspective, in this instance. Put the following up onto an OHP or flip chart, or provide copies of the words for everyone:

- You are having tea with two friends. You love cakes, and there are only two cream cakes left. What do you do?
- There is a lot of washing up, and no dishwasher. There are five adults in the house. What do you do?
- The garage door is banging late at night. There are four adults in the house. What do you do?

There may well be some funny answers to the storylines above. Listen to some of the results. Point out that as we tried to 'look after number one' so that we got the cake, or didn't do the washing up, etc. this is the way we should be looking after other people. Loving others, in essence, means putting them before ourselves.

☐ *Optional*

Gather the children together and look at whom we might consider to be 'our neighbour'. Draw concentric circles showing the way we relate to different people, e.g. ourselves, our immediate family, our wider family, our friends, those in our street, people in our country, those in the world. Who of these might be considered our neighbours?

BIBLE SUNDAY (OR LAST AFTER TRINITY)

The idea of the 'Day of the Lord' is explored to help prepare us for the day when God will come to judge us.

Nehemiah 8.1–4a (5–6) 8–12
Colossians 3.12–17
Matthew 24.30–35

- Group 1: Bibles, frieze paper and paint.
- Group 2: Copies of pictures depicting the 'Day of the Lord', Bibles.

- Group 3: Musical instruments, particularly percussion, Bibles.
- Group 4: A piece of music that reflects the subject, Bibles.
- Group 5: A4 paper and pens, Bibles.
- Group 6: Bibles, scissors, selection of different colours and textures of cloth.

☐ *Starter*

Carry out some research into the phrase 'the Day of the Lord', by setting up some of the following groups. More than one group could look at the same subject. Appoint leaders in the week beforehand to gather the tools needed for each group. Note that 'the Day of the Lord' is sometimes called 'the Second Coming of Christ' by Christians, or 'the coming of the Son of Man'.

Group 1

Read Amos 5.15–20; Joel 2.1–3; Joel 2.27–28; 1 Thessalonians 5.2–5; and Matthew 24.30–35 as a group, and discuss what kind of a scene this shows. Then as a group paint a mural to reflect the images. Use frieze paper or the back of a roll of wallpaper. As a group decide what the picture should show, and what colours should predominate. Allocate different areas to different people, and all work on it together. It would probably be easier to work on the floor, but trestle tables (or pasting tables) could be used.

Group 2

In the week beforehand gather a large number of copies of pictures showing 'the Day of the Lord'. Art books may show classical thoughts on this theme, and a good library should be able to help. Read Amos 5.15–20; Joel 2.1–3; Joel 2.27–28; 1 Thessalonians 5.2–5; and Matthew 24.30–35 as a group, and explore what they mean to each person. Now look at the pictures gathered. How do they reflect the thoughts of the group. Which pictures best reflect the group's thoughts and why?

Group 3

Gather a number of musical instruments, particularly percussion instruments. Perhaps a local school might be able to help. If possible this group needs to meet outside the main meeting room. Read Amos 5.15–20; Joel 2.1–3; Joel 2.27–28; 1 Thessalonians 5.2–5; and Matthew 24.30–35 and discuss what might be expected to happen at 'the Day of the Lord'. As a group plan and create a piece of music that reflects some of the group's thoughts.

Group 4
Find a piece of music that reflects the subject in the week before the service. If possible this group probably needs to meet outside the main meeting room. Read Amos 5.15–20; Joel 2.1–3; Joel 2.27–28; 1 Thessalonians 5.2–5; and Matthew 24.30–35 and discuss what might be expected to happen at 'the Day of the Lord'. As a group plan and create a dance to explore the theme of 'the Day of the Lord'.

Group 5
Read Amos 5.15–20; Joel 2.1–3; Joel 2.27–28; 1 Thessalonians 5.2–5; and Matthew 24.30–35. As a group brainstorm onto a sheet of large paper all the words that come into the minds of those in the group when they think of 'the Day of the Lord'. Create a large piece of collage on the theme, using as many of the brainstormed words as desired. Give the collage a title.

Group 6
Read Amos 5.15–20; Joel 2.1–3; Joel 2.27–28; 1 Thessalonians 5.2–5; and Matthew 24.30–35 and discuss what might happen when 'the Day of the Lord' occurs. As a group create some mime to explore the event.

 □ *Comment*

To the Jew the notion of 'the Day of the Lord' was well understood. It was to be the time when God would intervene in history. It would be a time of judgement for every man and woman. Jesus says it will come unexpectedly; there will be no warning, although the wise man will see the warning signs and be ready.

There is some confusion over whether 'the Day of the Lord' is the same as the Second Coming of Christ, and the different phrases are sometimes used interchangeably. At this time it was expected that Jesus would return to judge his people. Although the 'Day of the Lord' would be a time of great terror, nevertheless for God's people who had remained faithful it would be a time of joyful reunion.

Although many of the earliest Christians believed that Jesus would return in their lifetime we do know that God's time is not our time, and we still wait for his return. We too should be alert and awake, for Jesus may return at any time.

 □ *Conclusion*

Hear back from all the groups. Look at the collage and artwork, watch the dance and mime, and listen to the music group. Some of this could occur naturally in the remainder of the service, e.g. the dance could accompany a hymn, or the collage could be part of 'open-eyed' intercession.

THE FOURTH SUNDAY BEFORE ADVENT

An exploration of prophets and their work leads to an understanding of prophecy in relation to Jesus, and helps to identify their role in today's society.

Micah 3.5–12
1 Thessalonians 2.9–13
Matthew 24.1–14

- Bibles and texts.
- Paper and pens.

☐ *Starter*

Carry out as much study as possible on prophets and prophecy in the Old Testament. Appoint leaders the week beforehand and allocate a prophet to them, and agree some work that their group might do. Each group will need Bibles. For example:

1 What or who is a prophet?

Look at the following readings. Using a large sheet of paper and a fat pen list what things the prophets have in common regarding their call and their work. Compare this with Moses, who is considered to be the first major prophet.

Moses: Exodus 3.1–10; 3.10–15; 18.19.
Jeremiah: 1.1–10; 1.13–16; 1.17–19; 7.3–7; 22.1–6a.
Micah: 1.1–3; 1.8; 3.1–3; 6.9–11.
Jonah: 1.1–3; 3.1–3a; 3.6–9.
Ezekiel: 1.1–3; 1.4, 26–28a, 2.1–5; 3.1–3; 5.1–4; 8.1; 13.1–3; 14.1–5; 31.1–2; 39.1–3.

2 What titles or names are used for prophets, and what do you think they mean?

Look up the following readings. Using a large sheet of paper and a fat pen list what names are used for prophets.

Deuteronomy 33.1; Joshua 1.1–2; 1 Samuel 2.27; 9.6, 9—18–19; 17.1 Kings 13.1; 2 Kings 4.9; 17.13b; 23; 21.10; 1 Chronicles 9.22; Ezra 9.11; Isaiah 30.10; Jeremiah 7.25.

3 What is the work of a prophet?

Look up the readings and write down on a large sheet of paper, with a fat pen, all that you can find out about the work of a prophet.

> 1 Kings 17.17–24; 18.1, 17–45, 36
> Isaiah 2.1–2, 5; 30.6–9
> Jeremiah 3.22a; 10.6–7; 13.15–16
> Hosea 6.1–3; 14.1–2
> Joel 1.13
> Zephaniah 1.14
> Micah 4.1–4

4 What are the differences between true and false prophets?

Look at these readings, first, to see the difficulties that faced people in deciding whether a prophet was true or false. Make notes of all that you can find out on a large sheet of paper with a fat pen.

> 1 Kings 22.5–28 and Jeremiah 28.1–17
> False prophets can be divined as follows: Deuteronomy 13.1–4; 18.20–22; Jeremiah 23.13–17, and 21–22.
> True prophets prophesy the following: Deuteronomy 18.18–22; Ezekiel 12.28b.

5 Find out more about the last prophets.

Find out what you can about the prophecies of Anna, Simeon, Elizabeth, Mary and John the Baptist, and make notes on a large sheet of paper with a fat pen.

> John: Matthew 11.13–15
> Elizabeth: Luke 1.41–45
> Mary: Luke 1.46–55
> Zechariah: Luke 1.67–79
> Simeon: Luke 2.25–35
> Anna: Luke 2.36–38
> John: Matthew 11.13–15; Mark 6.17–29; Luke 1.5–25, 39–45, 57–80; 3.1–20, 21–22; John 1.6–9, 19–23, 29–37

□ *Comment*

Jesus teaches his disciples about the time that is to come after his death. He predicts the coming of the fall of Jerusalem which occurs in AD 70, and he speaks of his Second Coming to them. They ask him what signs will occur; how they will know that the time of his coming is imminent. He warns them not to be led astray by those promising to be the Messiah, or those who pretend to come in his name. He also warns them of those who will be false prophets and who will lead people astray.

As we have seen there are some important lessons to be learnt from the Old Testament. There was a very real problem over who was deemed to be a true prophet and who was a false one. The people needed to know how they could tell the two apart. For the consequences of following the wrong prophet could be appalling. God would not listen to such an excuse.

Things are not very different today. False prophets still occur. They call us to ignore God's wishes and follow the ways of the world. They call us to put all our energies into our work or even our family, and place the things of God second. They call us to ignore the injustices all around us. We need to apply the most basic rule of all, and ask ourselves, 'Is this what God would want?' When we test things against what God wants, it is usually possible to see if such people represent God or not.

☐ *Conclusion*

Hear back from all the groups. Place the large sheets of paper up on the wall and encourage people either to look at them, or ask someone from each group to speak about the aspect of prophets or prophecy they have been researching.

☐ *Optional*

Gather the large sheets together and write up the information into a small book on prophets and prophecy. Make the book available to the congregation as necessary.

THE THIRD SUNDAY BEFORE ADVENT

Christians are reminded of the need to be alert, always waiting for the coming of the Kingdom of God, and to do this with patience.

Wisdom of Solomon 6.12–16 or Amos 5.18–24
1 Thessalonians 4.13–18
Matthew 25.1–13

- Chinese sticks.
- Packs of cards.
- Instructions for 'rock, paper and scissors'.
- Newspapers and scissors.
- OHP or flip chart.
- *Optional:* Bibles, readings from Pentecost 25.

☐ *Starter*

Explain that today you are going to look at a number of games that involve patience or alertness.

- Chinese sticks (where sticks are dropped and participants try to pick up one stick at a time without moving any of the others).
- Build a house of cards.
- Play 'rock, paper and scissors': Each hits their open hand with their fist three times, and then makes one of the following signs:
  – clenched fist = rock (rock blunts scissors so wins)
  – open flat hand = paper (paper can cover and wrap rock so wins)
  – two open fingers = scissors (scissors cut paper and therefore wins)
- Flying fish: Cut fish shapes out of newspapers, and then use rolled up newspapers to flap behind the fish (without touching them). Hold a race with a number of others.
- I went to the Himalayas and I took with me a tent . . . (repeat around the group, each adding another item needed for the trip to the Himalayas, so that the group finally have to remember a long list of items).

☐ *Comment*

Jesus tells the disciples the parable of the bridesmaids waiting for the arrival of the bridegroom, to teach them about his Second Coming, and how they are to prepare themselves. Not knowing when the bridegroom will arrive, since the custom was to try and catch the bridal party unawares, the wise bridesmaids have prepared their lamps by filling them with oil. The foolish bridesmaids, though, are unprepared having run out of oil. They are forced to go and find more, and so miss the arrival of the bridegroom.

The disciples are to learn from the example of the wise bridesmaids, that they should be prepared for the coming of God's kingdom. Jesus may return at any time and they are to be ready and waiting, not caught unprepared. They need to have patience in the long wait before them, yet they must be alert for the signs of his coming.

Christians too need to hone all their skills of preparation, patience, and alertness to be ready to greet Jesus when he returns. If we get too caught up in the things of this world, then we shall not be prepared. If we become too involved with our family or friends we will be side-tracked from the things of God, and will not be prepared. Or if we fail to develop an ongoing relationship with our heavenly Father, then again we shall not be prepared when he comes to judge the world.

☐ *Conclusion*

Ask the congregation how, as Christians, we can prepare for Jesus' return. As a whole congregation come up with some helpful suggestions. Place these onto a flip chart or OHP.

☐ *Optional*

Set up a number of groups to look at any of the following:

- *Prayer*: Create some prayers to put into a booklet, on the theme of 'The Coming of Christ'. You might want to look up some of the kingdom prophecies (see Pentecost 25).
- *Parables*: Study some of the kingdom parables: Matthew 13.24–30, 31–32, 33, 44, 45–46, 47–50. How can these help us to be prepared for the coming of Christ, today?
- Create an 'Exercise Plan for Christians', or 'Ten Actions to get a Christian fit', for example:

  Pray every morning.

  Read a passage from my Bible daily.

  Read the newspaper or listen to the news each day, and use in prayer, etc.

THE SECOND SUNDAY BEFORE ADVENT

Christians are given different talents by God and are expected to use them for the growth of the Kingdom.

Zephaniah 1.7, 12–18
1 Thessalonians 5.1–11
Matthew 25.14–30

- Pretend money.
- A4 or A3 paper and fat pens.
- A4 paper and felt-tip pens or coloured pencils.
- Pencils.
- OHP or flip chart and pens.

☐ *Starter*

Give everyone in the congregation some pretend money. In the week beforehand create some fake money on a sheet and photocopy. Ideally it would be good to create a number of different notes, e.g. 50 'talents', 10 'talents' and 5 'talents'. The money can be given fairly randomly to individuals, or to groups if preferred. However, each group needs to know how much money it has had initially.

If desired, divide the congregation up into groups, but the work could be done by individuals if preferred.

First, ask each person or group to decide what knowledge and abilities they have which might be useful to someone else. For example some of the following might be considered 'saleable':

- Ability to draw or paint.
- Ability to sail a boat.
- Ability to ski.
- Ability to design.
- Knowledge of animals or birds.
- Knowledge of the human body, or of nursing.
- Knowledge of how to bring up a child.
- Knowledge of plants and gardening.

When this has been decided, write down the assets of the individual or group onto a sheet of paper. The person or a member of the group should now go and stand in the 'market-place'. The 'market-place' is somewhere that other groups can go to negotiate help. The negotiation should involve money and time, e.g. 'I will give you X pounds if you can spend two minutes drawing an outline picture of a bird for us.'

Now give each group a task from the group below. Inform them that they can receive up to £50 for their completed task, depending on how well they achieve the task.

- Prepare the designs for a wonderful garden suitable for a family with children. The plan should be as professionally drawn as possible, and should include the names of plants to be used. The group may wish to effect a trade with someone who has drawing skills, or knowledge of plants and gardens.
- Create a worksheet for children to look at birds in their gardens. Make sure you provide the answers to the questions. The worksheet should include a knowledge of the kind of birds that will appear at that time of the year, something about their feeding or nesting habits, and a picture of at least one or two birds. The group may wish to effect a trade with someone who knows something about birds or who can draw a bird.
- Create a sheet of exercises to help people recovering from injuries (to any part of the body) to get back to mobility. The worksheet is to include drawings of the exercises involved. The group may wish to effect a trade with someone who knows something about exercises, about injuries to the body, or who can draw.

- Create a sheet of modern games for children to play. The games may include the use of a ball or skipping rope, but no other implement. They can be for one child, or for a group. The sheet should include drawings to explain how to play the games. The group might want to effect a trade with some children to find out more about the games played now, and may wish to involve someone who can draw.
- Create a sheet of instructions for a beginner to learn to sail a small boat. The instructions should include diagrams or drawings to help the beginner, as well as the correct terminology. The group might want to effect a trade with someone who sails and with someone who can draw.
- Create a sheet of instructions for a beginner to learn to ski. The instructions should include information on the correct clothing and skis needed, as well as diagrams or drawings on how to ski. The correct terminology should be used. The group might want to effect a trade with someone who knows how to ski, and with someone who can draw.

The task now is for each person (or each group) to complete their task, if necessary through trade in the market place. They are to aim to earn as much money (i.e. 'talents') as an individual, or for the group, as possible.

□ *Comment*

The first thing to notice about the parable of the talents, is that although the master hands over all his property to his slaves he does not given equal quantities to the slaves. One is given five talents, another is given two talents, and another one talent.

In the same way God does not give each of us the same abilities (or talents). Each of us receives a different share. However, although we are given a different share of gifts we are expected to use them to the best of our ability. The only sin is not to use them. The slave who buries his talents and produces the same amount when his master returns is castigated as 'wicked and lazy'. This slave was probably thought to represent the Pharisees and Sadduccees who wanted everything to stay exactly as the law of Moses decreed, and who found Jesus' message of love and forgiveness impossible to accept. But it also has a message for us today. It reminds us that it is a sin not to use God's gifts. We are to increase them and to use them for work in his kingdom.

Lastly, it is important to notice that although the two servants increase their talents through hard work they are not congratulated and allowed to sit back. Their master gives them more responsibility and more work as a reward. In God's world reward is to continue the work in his kingdom.

□ *Conclusion*

Spend a moment or two listening to what happened, and finding out which person or group has earned the most money. Then find out how many people thought they had nothing saleable to offer. Is this in fact true? Can the congregation come up with other talents that are desirable, but perhaps were not used in this exercise, e.g. concern for others, praying for others, repairing cars, visiting, singing, listening, cooking, etc. List these on an OHP or flip chart. How might people use these gifts in the real world to further God's kingdom?

CHRIST THE KING

Ezekiel 34.11–16, 20–24
Ephesians 1.15–23
Matthew 25.31–46

- OHP or flip chart, and pen.
- Information on different church activities, if desired.

□ *Starter*

Divide the congregation into small mixed-aged groups of four or five people. Their task is to decide which of the following categories their church helps. It may be that as a church they help one or two categories in a number of ways, and they should list all of these. Put the following categories up on a flip chart or OHP:

- Feeding the hungry.
- Giving the thirsty drink.
- Welcoming the stranger.
- Clothing the naked.
- Looking after the sick.
- Caring for prisoners.
- .... (Is there another category that should be added to this list?)

Remind the congregation that some of these categories may have physical and spiritual aspects (e.g. food).

□ *Comment*

In today's Gospel reading we have heard a parable about giving. It is sometimes called the parable of the sheep and goats. God will judge us according to what we give. It is not that we are asked to give thousands of pounds to help those around us. Rather we are to give as generously as we can in small, practical ways. We are to care for the sick, feed the hungry, and visit those in prison. We are not to make judgements about whom we will care for or feed, neither are we to only help those on our doorstep. We are simply to offer care for those in need, wherever they are, or whatever their circumstances. In doing so, Jesus says, we are caring for God himself.

Jesus also warns us that when we refuse to help another person, we are refusing to help God himself, and we will be judged by him in due course according to the judgement that we made.

This parable should not worry us, so much as give us hope. Whatever our abilities or talents (*or whatever our income*), we are all capable of doing something for those around us who need help. God calls us to love our neighbour in practical ways, whether that neighbour is somewhere far away in prison (and who might value a letter, perhaps through Amnesty's write a letter scheme), or someone who is unwell across the road. As individuals, and as a church, we are called to give of our time, our talents, and our money, as each is able.

□ *Conclusion*

Gather together on an OHP or flip chart the suggestions that come from all the different groups. Then invite someone to come forward from each group. Identify them by name, and ask them for a sentence or two on their current work. You will need to watch the time at this point. Now encourage those who might not be involved in any of the work to think about speaking and becoming involved.

Lastly, look at the gaps, if there are some. Why is the church not involved in any of these areas (perhaps because of logistics, i.e. there is no prison nearby), and can this be remedied?

□ *Optional*

Create displays for the following week (so as not to alert everyone about the theme before this service) and encourage people to find out more about each aspect of Jesus' instructions.

□ *Optional*

Alternatively, have information on each church group available, this week, for anyone who asks.

□ *Optional*

Children might prefer to work together, to identify work that they could do as a group to help others.

APPENDIX

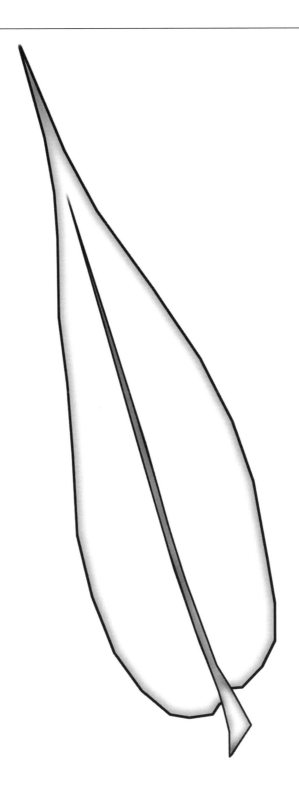

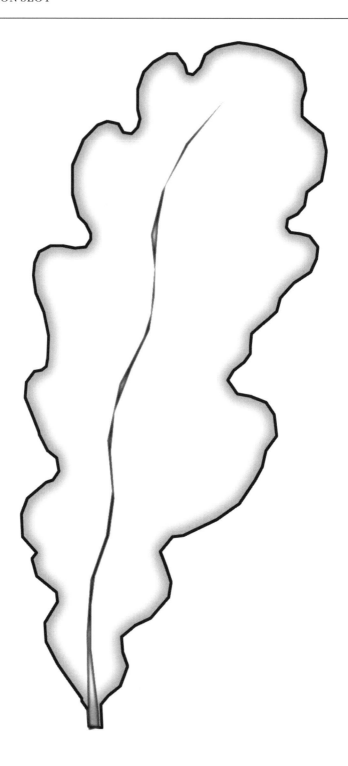

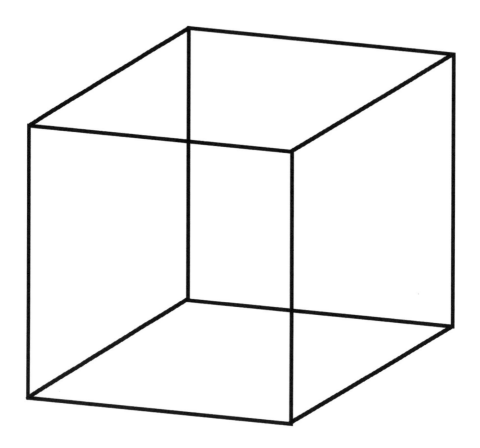

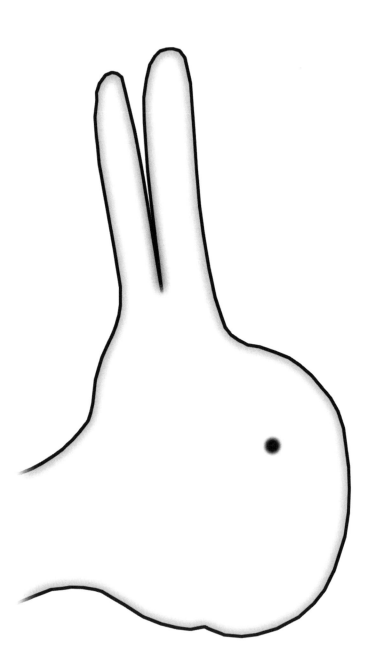

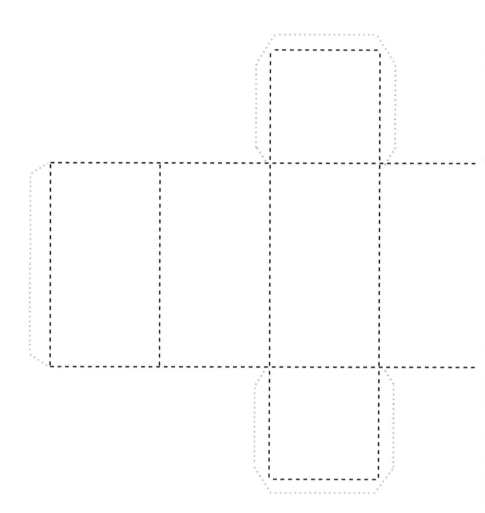